"URGENT! Read this book. Take notes. Take action. If you work for a nonprofit, you don't have to do every single thing these seasoned authors have to share, but you certainly have to know what you're missing. To do otherwise is malpractice."

—**Seth Godin,** author, *Linchpin*

"*The Networked Nonprofit* is a must-read for any nonprofit organization seeking innovative, creative techniques to improve its mission and better serve its communities."

—**Diana Aviv,** president and CEO, Independent Sector

"The Internet means never having to ask permission before trying something new; in *The Networked Nonprofit,* Fine and Kanter show nonprofits how to harness this flexibility to pursue their missions in partnership with two billion connected citizens."

—**Clay Shirky,** author, *Here Comes Everybody: The Power of Organizing Without Organizations*

"*The Networked Nonprofit* uniquely describes the historical context and the current challenges that compel nonprofit leaders to work in networked ways and offers easy steps to help users exploit the potential of social media and 'working wikily.'"

—**Stephanie McAuliffe,** director, organizational effectiveness, The David and Lucile Packard Foundation

"A must-read for nonprofit leaders who want to change their organizations from the inside out by embracing the power of social networks."

—**Charlene Li,** founding partner, Altimeter Group, author, *Open Leadership,* and coauthor, *Groundswell*

"This is a perfect handbook for those who want to leapfrog their current limitations of understanding and find real-world applications of technology to extend their mission."

—**Michele Nunn,** CEO, Points of Light Institute, and cofounder, HandsOn Network

"Kanter and Fine provide the 'Google Maps' for nonprofits so they can harness social media to kick butt and change the world."

—**Guy Kawasaki,** cofounder, Alltop.com, and former chief evangelist of Apple

"The preeminent experts in social media for social good, Beth Kanter and Allison Fine provide an excellent guide for helping nonprofits become more effective and nimble in this new, highly networked world."

—**Jean Case,** CEO and cofounder, Case Foundation

"Allison Fine and Beth Kanter have done an amazing job of bringing their experience and expertise to a readable technology book that will help non-techie decision makers understand how to use new technologies to move their organizations forward."

—**Marnie Webb,** co-CEO, TechSoup Global

"Social media are deeply changing the way people relate to one another, in business, politics, and the nonprofit world. *The Networked Nonprofit* gets you up to date on how nonprofit workers can use social media to help their organizations help their communities."

—**Craig Newmark,** founder, Craigslist

"Whether you're an early technology adopter or a lagging Luddite, there's something in here of value for anyone seeking to create greater impact. This book is a must-read for those serious about social change."

—**Heather McLeod Grant,** consultant, The Monitor Institute, and
  author, *Forces for Good: The Six Practices of High-Impact Nonprofits*

"Social media isn't about Twitter or Facebook, it's about a whole new way for nonprofits to create social change. Kanter and Fine have had their fingers on the pulse of this change and reveal what it means for you in a book that is smart, clear, and even entertaining."

—**Holly Ross,** executive director, NTEN: The Nonprofit Technology Network

"Don't just pick this book up and think you'll get a few tips. This is raw, mind-changing, and not likely to let you put it down right away."

—**Chris Brogan,** author of *Social Media 101*, and blogger at [chrisbrogan.com]

"Social media have changed everything. Now what? Buy this book for all the answers. It shows how to embrace this new world, navigate it with confidence, and harness its collective power to accelerate social change. Your cause will flourish with this guide in your hands."

—**Katya Andresen,** COO, Network for Good, and author, *Robin Hood Marketing*

"*The Networked Nonprofit* provides compelling motivation and practical coaching to nonprofit leaders so that even the most reluctant can join in the game. Vivid real-life stories illustrate the range of emerging opportunities while concrete examples of low-cost, low-risk experiments provide a bridge to action."

—**Jill A. Schumann,** president and CEO, Lutheran Services in America

"Kanter and Fine underscore that social media aren't a fad or trend or even a new Web site to discover; rather, they are the means of communicating, convening, building communities, and creating change in society today and tomorrow. Networked nonprofits are our tomorrow."

—**Sharna Goldseker,** vice president, The Charles and Andrea Bronfman Foundation

"Part manual, part manifesto, Kanter and Fine's guide for nonprofits shows how to embrace the future. It is packed with step-by-step guidelines and success stories so you know you are not alone. Read it, then get engaged in the power of networks."

—**Larry Blumenthal,** head of Social Media, Robert Wood Johnson Foundation

"*The Networked Nonprofit* takes social media beyond the marketing and IT departments of philanthropy—it's a book every board member and executive director should read, not just for great stories of how to use social media well, but because Allison Fine and Beth Kanter convincingly answer the question Why?"

—**Tom Watson,** author, *CauseWired: Plugging In, Getting Involved, Changing the World*

The Networked Nonprofit

CONNECTING WITH SOCIAL MEDIA

TO DRIVE CHANGE

Beth Kanter
Allison H. Fine

Foreword by
Randi Zuckerberg
Director of Marketing
Facebook

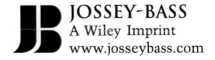

JOSSEY-BASS
A Wiley Imprint
www.josseybass.com

Published by Jossey-Bass
A Wiley Imprint
989 Market Street, San Francisco, CA 94103-1741—www.josseybass.com

Jossey-Bass books and products are available through most bookstores. To contact Jossey-Bass directly call our Customer Care Department within the U.S. at 800-956-7739, outside the U.S. at 317-572-3986, or fax 317-572-4002.

Jossey-Bass also publishes its books in a variety of electronic formats. Some content that appears in print may not be available in electronic books.

Library of Congress Cataloging-in-Publication Data

Kanter, Beth, date.
  The networked nonprofit: connecting with social media to drive change/Beth Kanter, Allison H. Fine.
    p. cm.
  Includes bibliographical references and index.
  ISBN 978-0-470-54797-7 (pbk.)
  1. Nonprofit organizations. 2. Social networks. I. Fine, Allison H., date. II. Title.
  HD62.6.K36 2010
  658′.044—dc22

                                                                      2010012745

Printed in the United States of America
FIRST EDITION

PB Printing   10 9 8 7 6 5 4 3 2 1

CONTENTS

FIGURES AND TABLES

FIGURES

TABLES

FOREWORD

The tragic earthquake in Haiti reverberated around the world on social media **channels** such as Facebook. Millions of people responded immediately by sending money by text message, sharing stories online, and organizing help for Haitians. Because of the spread of **social media**, we were able to respond in numbers and ways that would have been impossible just a few years ago.

We are social beings who thrive on connecting with one another and sharing our interests and issues. People love sharing their stories with one another. Sites such as Facebook enable us to connect with friends, new and old, all around the world and share our stories.

I truly enjoy my job at Facebook, where I focus on politics, nonprofits, and news and current events. We get to witness firsthand the conversations people are having around the world about important topics and events. There are more than 350 million people connecting with one another on Facebook, posting updates, sharing photos and videos, and promoting causes they are passionate about. What makes Facebook so powerful is that an individual can share content with his or her friends, who in turn share it with their friends—and in just a short time, a large number of people can come together around a common interest in a truly global conversation.

Let's look at some of the interesting ways people have used Facebook for breast cancer awareness and action. A few years ago, a Facebook user named Eric Ding used Facebook to ask friends to donate money for breast cancer research. Eric is a researcher at Brigham and Women's Hospital in Boston. Eric's friends supported his cause and shared the message with their friends. In a few months, he had over 2.2 million people signed on to support his efforts. By the end of 2009, Eric's cause had 5.5 million friends and over $135,000 to support breast cancer research. And in January 2010, a grassroots movement sprang up on Facebook where women suddenly began updating their status update with just one word, their bra color, to promote breast cancer awareness. Friends shared this message: "List the color of your bra in your FB status, just the color, nothing more. Then send this msg to your girlfriends too . . . no men. The point is to see how far we can spread breast cancer awareness . . . and make the men wonder what's up." Within a few hours, hundreds of thousands of people had updated their Facebook status and shared it with their network. This caught the attention of the national media, and everyone from CNN to *The Wall Street Journal* to ABC News reported on the effect of "the bra-vado."

And that's just one cause. Thousands of people use sites like Facebook every day to share their passion for causes, ranging from women's issues and illiteracy to the genocide in Darfur, to raise money and awareness. And it's not just young people—one of the fastest growing demographics on Facebook in 2009 was women over fifty! I've watched the amazing energy that people put into their causes online, and we've seen dozens of creative ideas and successful implementations, but I also know that it's only the beginning: we've only seen the tip of the iceberg when it comes to using social media channels for social change. And that's why I was so excited when Beth and Allison told me about this book, *The Networked Nonprofit*, because I know so many nonprofits and people who want to help, and who would benefit from hearing the authors' thoughts and ideas on putting the pieces together to be more effective solving social problems.

The power of social media to connect people, build relationships, and allow anyone, anywhere, to share their passions and interests, is amazing. But leveraging the power of social media isn't always intuitive for nonprofits. *The Networked Nonprofit* provides a framework for understanding how nonprofit organizations can become more open and connected and use social media more effectively for their causes. The first section of this book is really important because it focuses on ways that nonprofits and their leaders need to think and work differently to best use social media. The second section focuses on all the things that nonprofits can do once they embrace social media and open themselves up on channels like Facebook. That's when I get really excited about the new, fun, and creative ways that people can participate in to change the world for the better!

One of the most amazing aspects of the Internet and the Web is that there are simply no boundaries. There are no limits for who can participate. Whereas in the past, there were only two ways to get involved (donate money or donate time), now there are dozens of ways in which people can support the organizations they care about using social tools: updating their Facebook status about a cause, organizing a fundraising event, writing a blog post, producing and sharing a video, and many more. We are all learning together how to use social media well for causes, and there is so much value in sharing our successes and failures in this space. That's why *The Networked Nonprofit* is so important, because it helps everyone learn how to work together to leverage social media for social causes, to make a tremendous, positive impact on the world.

Palo Alto, California
April 2010

Randi Zuckerberg
Director of Marketing
Facebook

To our husbands, Walter and Scott,

and children, Harry, Sara, Maxwell, Zachary, and Jackson,

whose patience we needed to write this book

and whose love we need to get through life.

PREFACE

For most of the past decade we have had the privilege of witnessing and participating in nonprofit organizations' adoption and use of social media tools such as e-mail, **blogs**, and Facebook. We feel honored to be a part of this unfolding narrative and contribute to the genesis of an entirely new field.

We have both spent our entire careers working in, for, and with nonprofit organizations. So we well understood nonprofit leaders' trepidation as social media use began to gain traction. Their hesitation was based on two assumptions. The first was that the tools were the latest faddish craze created by and for kids. The second was that by using social media and opening up one's organization to the Wild West of the Web and **social networks**, an organization would damage its reputation and ability to control its own destiny. Neither assumption is true.

Social media will not fade away. It will continue to grow and become even more ingrained in how we live and work. As the use of social media has grown, leaders' skepticism has shifted from resistance to concern that they are being left behind. The question for organizational leaders is no longer whether to embrace social media, but how to do it effectively.

As one nonprofit executive director recently told us, "I've been doing this work since the seventies and I'm not on Facebook yet, but [I] won't be relevant unless we move into this space. And we can't do that unless we use social media [and] be present on social networks. But I don't know where to begin." We have written this book to help her, and the millions of other staff people and board members of nonprofit organizations, make their way into this new, social world.

Since 2005, many older, venerable organizations—such as the American Red Cross, the Humane Society of the United States, the National Wildlife

Federation, Planned Parenthood Federation of America, and the American Cancer Society—have opened themselves up to the world through social media. These organizations are having conversations with large numbers of supporters (and detractors) while imaginatively using a variety of tools to enable more people's participation, more easily and inexpensively than ever before. The emergence of an enormous generation of young people—Gen Y, or Millennials—passionate about social causes is fueling the surge of interest in social change work. However, they are far less interested in supporting individual nonprofit organizations over time. The alternative for these digital natives is to use the social media toolkit on behalf of their causes outside of organizations as free agent activists. This presents a significant challenge for all organizations, but particularly for those still hesitating to embrace the culture of openness and connectedness that young people expect.

Nonprofit organizations face other difficulties as well. The plunging economic fortunes of the country have left many communities and nonprofit organizations struggling. Social problems such as hunger and illiteracy are too large and complex for any single organization to solve, yet the nonprofit sector is organized largely as stand-alone organizations. The gravitational pull of individual organizations to become bigger, more complex, and more risk averse puts them at odds with the simplicity and openness that powers social media.

We believe that one important way for organizations to overcome these barriers is to break out of their lonely silos and embrace social media. By doing so they become connected with a larger ecosystem of organizations and individuals eager to help. These Networked Nonprofits work *as* social networks, not just in them.

Of course, nothing is harder for people than changing how they think and behave. We know how tough it is to do something fundamentally different in our personal lives—to eat less chocolate, exercise more, stop yelling at the kids so much, or try out that new gadget. Now magnify this challenge to the level of an organization or community, and see how daunting it can appear.

The good news is the change doesn't have to jar you. Organizations can take the small steps that we outline in this book to start on the pathway to becoming more open and connected—a Networked Nonprofit.

And while the transition might not be easy or comfortable at first, everyone can do it. It just takes some practice, which is exactly what we have been doing for the last few years.

Beth started Beth's Blog in 2003 when many people were asking her the question, "What's a blog?" Today, it is one of the most popular and influential blogs for nonprofits. While writing this book, she was a visiting scholar at The David and Lucile Packard Foundation, where she studied the intersection of social media for external communications and network effectiveness. Over the six years she has written her blog, she has modeled public learning about how to use these tools, and helped shine a light on social media mavens and network weavers working in nonprofit trenches. She earned recognition from *BusinessWeek* magazine as one of the social media innovators of 2009.

In addition, in her capacity as a board member, Beth has volunteered her time to use social networks to support the work of the Sharing Foundation, an organization that takes care of children in Cambodia. Her accomplishments include being the first person ever to use Twitter for fundraising in 2007, winning the first Giving Challenge sponsored by the Case Foundation, and raising money to underwrite the college education of Leng Sopharath, an orphan from Kampong Speu orphanage, who started her senior year at Norton University as an accounting major. Beth also helped sponsor the first-ever blogging conference in Cambodia for three hundred Cambodian young people.

Since 2005, Allison has researched and written about nonprofit organizations' use of social media. She wrote *Momentum: Igniting Social Change in the Connected Age* (2006). Allison writes A. Fine Blog and hosts a monthly podcast for *The Chronicle of Philanthropy* on using social media for social change. She was one of the organizers of the Twitter Vote Report project just prior to the national election in 2008. The project enabled thousands of individuals to share their voting experiences, good and bad, with other people using their cell phones. This open source system was subsequently adopted for the presidential inauguration, as well as for use in elections in India and Iran.

Through our own experiences, and those of the hundreds of organizations and people we talk to online every day, we're learning how best to use social media tools for social change. We are finding and practicing ways to distribute work to enable more people to participate and shape it. We are learning how to communicate better, share ideas, give credit, and thank people for their efforts. And, naturally, we have made more than a few mistakes that we've shared with our networks as well.

We are in awe of the work that nonprofit staff, free agent activists, volunteers, donors, bloggers, and others do every day with such passion, energy, and selflessness, all to help heal the world. Our aim with this book is to celebrate their efforts, build on them, and encourage hesitant nonprofit leaders to join them online.

ABOUT THIS BOOK

We would like to share a few thoughts with our readers about this book. It is focused largely on efforts within the United States. Amazing work is happening around the world, of course, but our experiences come from our work mainly with U.S.-based organizations, which shapes our views and the content of this book.

The book begins with an introductory chapter, "Introducing Networked Nonprofits," which defines Networked Nonprofits and describes the social media revolution and the myths that have stopped too many nonprofit executives from engaging in it.

Chapter Two, "Nonprofit Challenges and Trends," provides the context for the urgent need for nonprofit organizations to transition into being Networked Nonprofits. The book is then divided into two parts: Part One, "How to Become a Networked Nonprofit," is focused on how organizations can become Networked Nonprofits, and Part Two, "What to Do as a Networked Nonprofit," is focused on what being a Networked Nonprofit will help them achieve.

The first part, "How to Become a Networked Nonprofit," encompassing Chapters Three through Seven, focuses on how organizations must operate to use social media successfully and effectively. Topics include Chapter Three, "Understanding Social Networks"; Chapter Four, "Creating a Social Culture"; Chapter Five, "Listening, Engaging, and Building Relationships"; Chapter Six, "Building Trust Through Transparency"; and Chapter Seven, "Making Nonprofit Organizations Simpler."

The second part, "What to Do as a Networked Nonprofit," describes the way organizations can work when structured this way. Chapter Eight, "Working with Crowds," looks at working with large numbers of people outside the organization to spread out the work. Chapter Nine, "Learning Loops," describes ways organizations can continuously monitor and improve their efforts involving social media. Chapter Ten, "From Friending to Funding," focuses on turning friends into funders using social media. And Chapter Eleven, "Governing Through Networks," outlines ways that organizations can use social media to reshape organizational governance.

Each chapter ends with Reflection Questions to help you start internal discussions about that chapter's topics. They are not intended to provide how-to steps for using specific social media tools, but we do list Additional Resources at the end of each chapter to facilitate that kind of learning. You can also reference the Glossary for definitions of social media tools mentioned in the book.

We encourage readers first to explore the ways that organizations have to structure themselves and the ways that their leadership should reorient themselves to their work and the world. However, we understand that some topics, such as working with crowds, are of particular interest; and readers should feel free to explore each chapter directly.

However, we ask for one thing in exchange: for organizational leaders anxious to jump to the *what* and *how* of social media, please practice using the tools yourselves. It's the only way to discover social media's power to change the way we think and work. We also hope you will trust the people within your organization to do the same, and encourage them to connect with the world in positive, creative ways.

April 2010

Beth Kanter
Los Altos, California

Allison H. Fine
Irvington, New York

ACKNOWLEDGMENTS

We are blessed with networks of people with amazing energy, creativity, and generosity of spirit who assisted in the development of the book. We are particularly grateful for the assistance of the amazing people who are working in the trenches of nonprofits, social media, and social change every day. They are our heroes. We have learned from them as they work every day to make the world a better place to live.

We'd like to thank the team at Jossey-Bass/Wiley for their assistance and support throughout this process. Jesse Wiley, Dani Scoville, Mickey Butts, Elizabeth Forsaith, and Xenia Lisanevich have shepherded our book with great care and vision. We love Julia Rocchi for her big hair and big mouth, but most of all we love her for her amazing editing skills.

We are enormously indebted to our expert content reviewers Geoff Livingston, Danielle Brigida, Brian Reich, and Micah Sifry for their time and thoughtful suggestions.

Beth would like to offer special thanks to The Sharing Foundation and in particular Dr. Hendrie, who has been her role model for working on social change and caring for children in Cambodia. Allison is also grateful for the work of Hope for Henry and is in awe of the courage and generosity of its founders Laurie Strongin and Allen Goldberg. We will donate proceeds from this book to these organizations.

We are appreciative of two foundations for their support of our work and learning over the last several years. The David and Lucile Packard Foundation, where Beth was a visiting scholar during 2009, provided an opportunity for thinking and writing and learning time that would not have been otherwise available. The staff and board members who were especially generous with their time and support include Julie Packard, Stephanie McAuliffe, Carol Larson, Chris DeCardy, Kathy Reich, Anastasia Ordonez, Catherine Afarian, Irene Wong, David Perper, Loretta

Gallegos, Gale Berkowitz, Liz Karlin, Matt Sharpe, Lois Salisbury, Eunice Delumen, Eugene M. Lewit, Linda Schuurmann Baker, Arron Jiron, Meera Mani, Jeff Sunshine, Liane Wong, Jenny Calixto Quigley, Musimbi Kanyoro, Kathy Toner, Walter Reid, Kai Lee, Jamie Dean, Lisa Monzon, Laura Sullivan, Sheila Direickson, and Sandra Bass. Also, thanks to the consultants and experts who work closely with Packard Foundation staff and grantees: Dan Cohen, Holly Minch, Jen Lamson, Kristin Grimm, Katherine Fulton, Diana Scearce, Heather McLeod Grant, Noah Flowers, Eugene Eric Kim, June Holley, Michael Patton, and many others.

The Case Foundation has also provided amazing opportunities over the past several years for us to conduct research and learn how nonprofit organizations are utilizing social media over a broader segment of the nonprofit sector than we could learn through our blogging. We would like to thank Steve and Jean Case, Ben Binswanger, Michael Smith, Kari Dunn Saratovsky, Brian Sasscer, Erich Broksas, Sokunthea Sa Chhabra, Eric Johnson, Megan Stohner, Kristin Ivie, and the rest of the staff for their support and encouragement as our projects together unfolded.

We wanted to give a special thanks to our nonprofit colleagues and the social media gurus who generously shared their knowledge, stories, and experiences to help shape this book. They include, but aren't limited to, Lucy Bernholz, Jake Brewer, Jonathon Colman, Peter Deitz, Qui Diaz, Laura Lee Dooley, Jon Dunn, Christine Egger, Jill Finalyson, Stephen Foster, Susan Granger, Wendy Harman, Humberto Kam, James Leventhal, Carie Lewis, David Neff, Chad Nelson, Adin Miller, Elizabeth Miller, Ellen Miller, Kivi Leroux Miller, Perli Ni, Ory Okolloh, Peggy Padden, Andrew Rasiej, Holly Ross, Nancy Scola, Suzanne Seggerman, Kristen Taylor, Susan Tenby, Marnie Webb, Rachel Weidinger, Deanna Zandt, Andrew Zolli, Ethan Zuckerman.

And a special thanks goes to the social media experts who shared their insights with us including Chris Brogan, Pete Cashmore, Steve Garfield, Seth Godin, Tara Hunt, Kami Watson Huyse, Avinash Kaushik, Shel Israel, Adina Levin, Charlene Li, Dave McClure, KD Paine, Rashmi Sinha, Tom Watson, Tamar Weinberg, and Randi Zuckerberg.

Finally, we would like to thank our blog readers and online friends who are participating in the ongoing conversation about using social media for social change. Thanks for sharing your experiences and ideas and allowing us to experiment and learn together with you. And thanks for sharing this exciting roller-coaster ride as we all build this new field together.

—*B. K. and A. H. F.*

THE AUTHORS

Beth Kanter is the author of Beth's Blog: How Nonprofits Can Use Social Media (http://www.bethkanter.org), one of the longest running and most popular blogs for nonprofits. Beth has authored chapters in several books, including *Managing Technology to Meet Your Mission: A Strategic Guide for Nonprofit Leaders*, edited by the Nonprofit Technology Network (Jossey-Bass/John Wiley & Sons, 2009). A much-in-demand speaker and trainer at nonprofit conferences, she has been invited to present at some of the leading social media industry conferences, including O'Reilly's Graphing Social Patterns, Gnomedex, SWSX, Blogher, and Podcamp. In 2009, she was named by *Fast Company* magazine as one of the most influential women in technology and as one of *BusinessWeek*'s "Voices of Innovation for Social Media." She is CEO of Zoetica (http://www.zoeticamedia .com) and is Visiting Scholar for Social Media and Nonprofits for The David and Lucile Packard Foundation. She lives with her husband, Walter, and two children, Harry and Sara, in California.

Allison H. Fine is the author of the award-winning book *Momentum: Igniting Social Change in the Connected Age* (Jossey-Bass/John Wiley & Sons, 2006). She is a senior fellow on the democracy team at Demos: A Network for Change and Action in New York City. In 2008, she published a paper on young people and activism commissioned by the Case Foundation called "Social Citizensbeta," and coedited a collection of essays, *Rebooting America: Ideas for Redesigning American Democracy for the Internet Age*, published by the Personal Democracy Forum (2008), about transformative ways to reinvent twenty-first-century democracy using new media tools. Allison hosts a monthly podcast for *The Chronicle of Philanthropy* called "Social Good" and writes her own blog, A. Fine Blog. She lives with her husband, Scott, and three sons, Max, Zack, and Jack, in the Hudson Valley of New York.

Introducing Networked Nonprofits

Surfers and other ocean enthusiasts share common characteristics of stubborn independence and rugged individualism. Like unherded cats, surfers do what they want to do when they want to do it. Any organization intending to organize them could only succeed by operating very differently from a traditional, top-down institution. And that's exactly what the Surfrider Foundation has done.

A handful of surfers founded the Surfrider Foundation in 1984 to protect oceans and beaches through conservation, activism, research, and education. They work with a variety of ocean enthusiasts including surfers, bodysurfers, bodyboarders, windsurfers, swimmers, divers, beachcombers, and ocean-loving families.

As of 2009, the organization had a budget of around $5 million and thirty staff people working at the national headquarters in San Clemente, California. Surfrider is an inside-out organization. It opens up its work to the world by sharing its strategic plan, annual reports, financial statements, audit reports, and tax forms. It encourages its staff to talk about the work: CEO Jim Moriarity and other staff are available for discussions on its Oceans Waves Beaches blog and on Twitter.

The organization's conservation work happens largely through their all-volunteer chapters. Surfrider doesn't dictate what the chapters do, but rather follows and supports them. The foundation is devoted to building meaningful relationships with supporters that go far beyond asking for donations. Taken in total, Surfrider resembles a social network rather than a traditional stand-alone organization. We call Surfrider and organizations like it **Networked Nonprofits**.

In 2008, the Surfrider network included over seventy Surfrider chapters located along the East, West, Gulf, Hawaiian, and Puerto Rican coasts. The organization had over fifty thousand paying members and many more thousands of local volunteers. In addition to the local chapters, several hundred groups and pages on Facebook were dedicated to Surfrider and its local chapters.

Each chapter works on what the organization calls "atom-based work" on land and "bit-based work" online. The atom-based work includes organizing beach cleanups, testing beach waters, and conducting local education programs. The bit-based work involves many conversations on a variety of social media channels such as Facebook and Twitter, sending out e-mail action alerts, and organizing events online (see Figure 1.1).

Surfrider has created a unique model of engagement to map the participation of volunteers from strangers to friends to supporters, members, activists, and leaders. The organization provides a variety of ways for people to participate at every level. Strangers and friends can buy T-shirts online and sign up for e-mail alerts. More involved supporters and members can download and listen to podcasts and organize local beach cleanups. Leaders can arrange to meet with elected officials to discuss legislation to protect the shorelines.

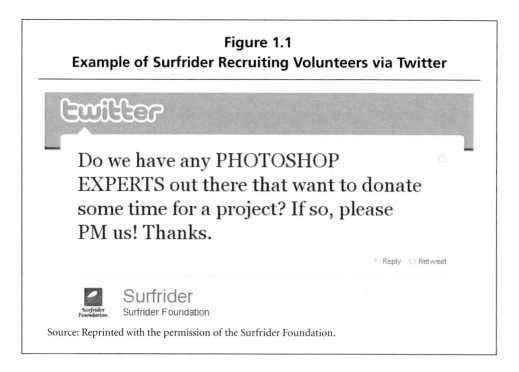

Figure 1.1
Example of Surfrider Recruiting Volunteers via Twitter

Do we have any PHOTOSHOP EXPERTS out there that want to donate some time for a project? If so, please PM us! Thanks.

Reply   Retweet

Surfrider
Surfrider Foundation

Source: Reprinted with the permission of the Surfrider Foundation.

Like the surfers, the chapters do what they want to do when they want to do it. The Foundation trusts their distributed network of people to work on its behalf without requiring constant oversight. Chad Nelson, Surfrider's environmental director, said that while this might annoy the lawyers, the national office rarely polices or intervenes with what the chapters are doing.

And it all works to engage people locally and energetically on behalf of the organization. In 2008, Surfrider had over 200 community outreach campaigns, over 900 local presentations of its Respect the Beach education program, over 8,000 beach water tests taken, and over 600 beach cleanups. Surfrider Chapter representatives attended over 125 meetings and events involving city, county, and state governments. In total, volunteers contributed over 145,000 volunteer hours.[1]

The Surfrider Foundation ignites the passions of thousands of ocean enthusiasts. In return, this network of participants shares their energy and enthusiasm for Surfrider with their own personal networks of friends, volunteers their time, and donates money to support the organization.

ABOUT NETWORKED NONPROFITS

Networked Nonprofits are simple and transparent organizations. They are easy for outsiders to get in and insiders to get out. They engage people in shaping and sharing their work in order to raise awareness of social issues, organize communities to provide services, or advocate for legislation. In the long run, they are helping to make the world a safer, fairer, healthier place to live.

Networked Nonprofits don't work harder or longer than other organizations, they work differently. They engage in conversations with people beyond their walls—lots of conversations—to build relationships that spread their work through the network. Incorporating relationship building as a core responsibility of all staffers fundamentally changes their to-do lists. Working this way is only possible because of the advent of social media. All Networked Nonprofits are comfortable using the new social media tool set—digital tools such as e-mail, blogs, and Facebook that encourage two-way conversations between people, and between people and organizations, to enlarge their efforts quickly, easily, and inexpensively.

We know nonprofit staffs often feel overburdened, with too much pressure on too few people to do too much. As we will discuss in Chapter Seven, "Making Nonprofit Organizations Simpler," nonprofits and the people within them have too much to do because they try to do too much as stand-alone organizations. Networked Nonprofits know their organizations are part of a much larger ecosystem of organizations and individuals that are all incredible resources for their efforts.

Networked Nonprofits are not afraid to lose control of their programs and services, their logos and branding, messages and messengers because they know that in return they will receive the goodwill and passion of many people working on their behalf. Working this way enables these organizations to reach many more people less expensively than they ever could working largely alone.

Some organizations such as the Surfrider Foundation, and others that we will discuss in this book, such as MomsRising and charity: water, are born as Networked Nonprofits. But being Networked Nonprofits is not just an accident of birth. Any organization can become one, and many are in the process of doing so. Venerable nonprofit organizations, such as the American Red Cross, the Humane Society of the United States, Planned Parenthood, and the American Cancer Society, are turning themselves inside out with great success. We will share their stories, struggles, and lessons throughout this book in order to encourage other organizations to become Networked Nonprofits.

But organizations are not the only entities powering **social change** in this new, connected world. Individuals—we call them *free agents*—combine their social media savvy with their passion for social causes to accomplish amazing things. Free agents' facility with social media gives them the power and tools that only organizations had just a few years ago. They have become integral parts of ecosystems within which nonprofit organizations work. While traditional organizations may bristle at their emergence, Networked Nonprofits naturally work with them toward common ends.

THE SOCIAL MEDIA REVOLUTION

Evolutions are incremental improvements of a product or idea. The newest Ford Mustang or iPod may be better iterations than previous versions, but they are still fundamentally the same product. When two teenagers, Shawn Fanning and Sean Parker, created the online music-sharing site Napster in 1999, they sparked a revolution. Power shifted away from music companies toward music listeners. For the first time, consumers had the ability to shape their own collection of songs any way they wanted, and perhaps more important, share these songs with the world online.

It wasn't legal, it still isn't, but it was inevitable given that millions of people could easily and inexpensively access and use the tools. Even if services such as iTunes slow down the free sharing of music files online, they will never erase it entirely. The genie has popped out of the bottle, and she won't be put back in. Social media are revolutionary in their power and reach.

In the 1980s, personal computers landed on everyone's desk and changed the way information was stored and organized. In the 1990s, the World Wide Web connected a universe of people and made information accessible. This century has seen the rise of the social graph; the relationships people are making and renewing using social media tools, particularly social networking sites, enable rapid, collective activity.

We define social media as the array of digital tools such as **instant messaging, text messaging,** blogs, videos, and social networking sites like Facebook and MySpace that are inexpensive and easy to use. Social media enable people to create their own stories, videos, and photos and to manipulate them and share them widely at almost no cost. Included in this book is a Glossary to provide more definitions of specific tools and processes.

Social media tools integral to nonprofits fall into three general categories of use:

- Conversation starters like blogs, YouTube, and Twitter
- Collaboration tools including wikis and Google Groups
- Network builders like social networking sites such as Facebook, MySpace, and Twitter

Social media are not a fad or a trend. With near-universal access to the World Wide Web in the United States, and the ubiquity of mobile phones and e-mail, the use of social media will only continue growing. Social media use is becoming ingrained in the way that people relate to one another and work together. In particular, social media are shaping the way that young people think, connect, engage, and work together.

We want to caution readers that knowing how to use social media well is not just about knowing which button to push. Technological wizardry shouldn't overshadow the truly revolutionary power of social media, which is its ability to connect people to one another and help build strong, resilient, trusting relationships. But the only way to understand this distinction is to use the toolset personally. There is no other way to fully understand the power of using social media to connect friends and strangers with common interests than to experience it personally. In other words: *Social media use is a contact sport, not a spectator sport.*

We also warn you that there is no universal rule about which tool will work under which circumstances for which people. Networked Nonprofits do not use just one tool. They use many tools to engage in different kinds of conversations with different groups of people.

More important, keep in mind that tools will come and go, but strategy sustains organizations. Choosing and using any specific tool is less important to organizational success than embracing the principles and strategies that make social media effective. Using social media is a way of being more than a way of doing.

Unfortunately, too many nonprofit organizations are losing ground today because they fear what might happen if they open themselves up to this new world. These organizations are crashing into this set-me-free world powered by social media, unprepared to become Networked Nonprofits. Many of these fears are unfounded. Let's begin by facing and overcoming the fears and myths about social media use that simply aren't true.

BUSTING THE SOCIAL MEDIA MYTHS

The array of social media tools look complex from the outside—a beeping, flashing, chattering din. Watching young people glide through the social media world with ease adds to the perception that social media is only for the technologically savvy or the young. Neither perception is true. But you don't have to take our word for it; we'll let Peggy Padden explain.

Fate dealt Peggy's family the cruelest blow when two of her three sons were born with a genetic blood disorder called Fanconi Anemia (FA), which leads to bone marrow failure. Her eldest son died after a failed bone marrow transplant, while her younger son is still fighting the disease. But by nature Peggy is a doer, so she energetically began to raise money for the Fanconi Anemia Research Fund to help find a cure for this terrible disease. She organized 5k runs/walks on Valentine's Day and golf tournaments as fundraisers in Portland, Oregon, where she lives.

In December 2007, Peggy saw an article in *PARADE* magazine about a new fundraising contest called America's Giving Challenge. The Case Foundation, the family philanthropy started by AOL founder Steve Case and his wife Jean, sponsored the Challenge. They encouraged individuals to join the Challenge by signing up online at *PARADE* magazine's site or on Facebook.

Over a fifty-day period, these individuals, or champions, competed to raise the largest number of people to give at least $10 each for their cause. The eight champions who raised the largest number of friends during the contest would win the money they raised, plus $50 thousand from the Case Foundation.

Peggy's reaction when she read the challenge description was, "That's a lot of money!" She decided to give it a try.

Peggy was the first to admit that all the newfangled technology tools—all of that "Face page stuff" in her words—was not meant for a fifty-year-old woman like her. She knew enough to get by, she thought. She read and sent e-mail, surfed the Web a bit, and was very excited when she learned how to cut and paste in a Word document. But that was it; she left the rest for her children. That is what made Peggy's success in America's Giving Challenge, a fundraising effort that hinged on using new social media tools like Facebook, such a huge surprise.

A few clicks on the *PARADE* magazine Web site and Peggy had registered her cause for the Challenge and added her name as the champion. "I was a beginner; I've never done anything like a **badge** before," she says. "I was able to figure it out except for the picture; I couldn't get it any bigger." She waited for her son to get home to fix the photo.

Once she set up the badge, Peggy began to do what she felt most comfortable doing: she e-mailed her family, friends, acquaintances, and the 250 families on the Fanconi Anemia **listserv** and asked them to become a friend to her cause and donate $10. It was a long shot, she said, but they could possibly win $50 thousand and that money would go toward our only hope for a cure for Fanconi Anemia. She also asked them to e-mail everyone they knew about the Challenge. And they did.

Word began to spread online about Peggy's cause. As she recalled, "That six degrees of separation part was right on. I would hear from someone who knew someone who knew someone who had e-mailed everyone they knew. It spread like wildfire."[2]

Her cause had gone **viral**, meaning friends of friends were doing things on her behalf without Peggy having to ask them to do so directly. To Peggy's astonishment, people she didn't know put the Fanconi Anemia cause up on their Facebook pages, on their blogs, and on MySpace. It was time for Peggy to put aside her fears and anxiety about social media and just jump into the mael-strom on Facebook and everywhere else the conversation about her cause was happening.

Peggy had no overall plan and no marketing budget. She and her friends just kept going and doing, and somehow it all worked. She wasn't quite sure what people were doing and saying on her behalf, but it didn't matter. The results were clear; many people were working on her behalf and moving their friends to sup-port her cause. Peggy provided constant e-mail updates to her friends, new and old, about how they were doing in the Challenge.

Peggy's efforts continued to pick up steam. She recalls: "At first they thought it was just another one of my crazy ideas and that we couldn't win. Then when we were number five we were so excited and checking the Web site to see where we were in comparison to the other charities. Wow, we thought, this really could happen!"

When the Case Foundation announced the winners of America's Giving Challenge, Peggy won second place. Her cause garnered 2,730 friends and $65,538, plus the $50,000 challenge grant for a grand total of $115,538.[3]

As Peggy proved, remembering a world before the Internet does not disqual-ify a person from using social media well. The data about social media usage are also proving this assumption wrong. According to the Pew Center for American Life and the Internet, the average age of Web users is mid-forties, the average age of Facebook users is climbing, and 95 percent of the population have mobile phones and use e-mail.[4]

The first myth that social media is just for kids has been busted. Let's con-tinue our social media myth busting:

- **Our constituents aren't online**. The old assumptions of a digital divide that makes access to technology in low-income communities difficult to over-come no longer hold. Although a gap of access persists, it is closing very rapidly, and the almost-universal mobile phone usage here and abroad will soon put this issue to rest. For a time, organizations will need to continue to reach out in traditional ways to constituencies with access problems or who are hesitant to use social media. But they should still prepare for a future where everyone is using social media.
- **Face-to-face isn't important anymore**. Nothing will ever substitute for the power of people meeting face-to-face. No amount of clicking, pinging, and

poking can build the trust that happens in a room between people—ever. Social media augments relationships built on land. It is important for organizations to avoid the social media zero-sum game, meaning the presumption that because some things happen online now, they don't happen on land anymore. Online and on-land activities augment one another; they have to in order for social change to happen.

- **Social media isn't core to our work**. It's difficult to imagine any organization engaged in social change where relationship building, conversations, and connections aren't core to their success. Social media strengthens these relationships and connections with people outside of an organization's walls.

- **Using social media is hard**. If social media tools were hard to use, they wouldn't be so widespread. As Clay Shirky wrote, "Communications tools don't get socially interesting until they get technologically boring."[5] But as with anything in life, mastering social media requires practice. Everyone needs to try the tools to understand why they are so powerful and important and to discover for themselves which ones they like and which work best for them.

- **Using social media is time-consuming**. Okay, this one is actually true. It does take time to use social media, particularly in the beginning when there is a learning curve to master. However, once the workflow becomes a habit, Networked Nonprofits accomplish more with less time. And ultimately, when people and organizations become better at working with their networks and learn how to distribute their work rather than assume all the heavy lifting, their overall workload will decrease.

As Peggy Padden learned, using social media is easy; but using it effectively for social change is challenging. It's important to understand exactly what social media can do for organizations, and then rethink how organizations could work by embracing it.

SOCIAL MEDIA POWERS SOCIAL NETWORKS FOR SOCIAL CHANGE

This book is built on a simple equation: Social Media Powers Social Networks for Social Change. When we discuss this equation with people working within nonprofit organizations, they sometimes miss the operative word: social. Their focus is on the gadgetry when it should be on embracing social ways of behaving.

This distinction is key not only to using social media, but also to effecting social change.

One constant in life is that human beings want and need to connect with one another in meaningful ways. These connections are made through social networks that are the conduits for the conversations that power social change. The job of nonprofit organizations is to catalyze and manage those conversations.

Forty years ago, it was commonplace for people to throw trash out of car windows as they sped down the highway. Today that's not acceptable behavior. The change didn't result from one person's or organization's efforts, or even one crying Native American in a television commercial. Change happened because individuals began to adjust their behavior based on the norms developed within their social circles. As friends, mothers, children, aunts, and cousins begin to change their behavior, so does everyone they know. Laws codify this behavior; they don't create it.

Conversations through social media include two-way discussions between people, and between people and organizations. Conversations also include sharing information online, like photographs, for friends or the broader public to see and comment on; writing a blog post that stirs a conversation in the comments section; and raising awareness of an issue on Facebook. Conversations are the lifeblood of social change efforts. Without them, people would not donate, protest, change their minds, or pass new laws.

We describe social media as **channels** in this book, meaning vehicles for conversations. Networked Nonprofits engage in conversations with people using multiple social media channels. We also define social change inclusively for this book. **Social change** means any effort by people and organizations to make the world a better place. It includes advocacy and direct service efforts, as well as conversations between people outside organizations about challenges that people and communities face. If the intention is to understand and fix problems, improve people's lives, or strengthen communities, we consider those efforts part of the broad spectrum of social change.

Conversations activate the natural creativity and passion that people bring to causes they care about. Just ask Peggy Padden how excited people are to help when given a chance. That's what Networked Nonprofits working as social networks and using social media can accomplish.

chapter TWO

Nonprofit Challenges and Trends

The rise of social media seemed to happen in an instant. One minute we were marveling at fax machines' speed, the next minute hundreds of millions of people are connecting with friends and sharing photos and news on Facebook. As discussed in the previous chapter, social media are revolutionary in their power to connect people, help them self-organize, and express themselves. But while social media power Networked Nonprofits, they aren't the only reason nonprofit organizations need to shift their focus from their individual organizations to their networks.

Other changes affecting individual organizations and the nonprofit sector as a whole are happening more slowly. They include a serious leadership crisis in addition to profound generational shifts and the rise of a new kind of social change agent that we call *free agents*. But these are challenges that can also be solutions, although they require people and nonprofit organizations to shift their thinking. In this chapter, we will discuss these challenges, their implications, and the ways that Networked Nonprofit organizations can help overcome them.

THE LEADERSHIP CRISIS

Over the past several decades, the nonprofit sector experienced spectacular growth in every measurable way. The number of nonprofit organizations in the United States rose over 30 percent from 1998 to 2008, from about 1.1 million to 1.5 million. The number of private foundations grew over 60 percent in that same period, from 70,000 to 115,000 organizations.[1]

In 2005, nonprofit organizations employed 12.9 million individuals, or approximately 9.7 percent of the U.S. economy—more than the financial activities sector employed at that time. And in 2008, nonprofits' total revenue was $307.65 billion.[2]

The centerpiece of this expansion has been the creation and growth of individual organizations, each with its own mission, staffs, and revenue needs. In *Diminishing Democracy: From Membership to Management in American Civic Life*, Theda Skocpol meticulously traces the rise of large nonprofit organizations and associations throughout American history. She describes the creation and growth of voluntary associations, which created value within local communities by training individuals with community organizing and leadership skills, bridging class divides through participation in common associations, and strengthening communities through direct support of people and communities in need.

Several important events in the second half of the twentieth century caused nonprofit organizations to turn inward and pull away from their own members and communities. First was the rise of professional staff. Hired as expert managers, staff had to prove themselves more adept at managing their organizations than the volunteers they replaced. Second, the number and size of private foundations that preferred to support professionally staffed organizations grew. Third, organizations began to define success as staff and budget growth to satisfy their staff, boards, and funders, which pressured individual organizations to raise more money. And finally, the advent of information technology enabled organizations to raise more money from more people through direct mail without having to interact with them personally.

The result was that "cause-oriented advocacy groups and professionally managed institutions offer[ed] wealthy and well-educated Americans a menu of opportunities to, in effect, hire experts to represent their values and interests in public life."[3] In their view, they didn't have to share how their organizations worked, what they chose to do, and how they did it with distant constituents.

The incessant pressure on professional nonprofit organizations to grow financially and programmatically forced organizations to consider everyone else competitors—a stumbling block when you're trying to address complex, difficult social problems. Nonprofit organizations stopped reaching beyond their borders to engage in real problem solving with other organizations and individuals. David Renz writes, "The scale of these complex problems [has] outgrown the capacity of our existing freestanding organizations to respond."[4]

Nonprofit organizations had become Sisyphean, laboring mightily to roll their organizations up the hill every day.

We are writing this book in the depths of the greatest economic recession in several generations. The unfettered growth so many organizations enjoyed over the past two decades has come to a screeching halt, with many downsizing and others closing their doors. But while it's heart wrenching to watch people and their communities suffer during a time of great need and uncertainty, nonprofit leaders cannot allow the recession to mask the fundamental flaws that they must address within their organizations.

Working alone against such large odds leads stand-alone organizations to send out a cacophony of urgent appeals for funds. These appeals are steeped in hyperbole, wearing people out over time. We are not implying that the appeals' subjects aren't real or pressing or heartbreaking, or that organizations don't need funds, but rather that operating at a constant state of panic exhausts people inside and outside those organizations. The habits and structures of these freestanding organizations are fundamentally incompatible with being Networked Nonprofits.

Of course, not all nonprofit organizations work in solitude, keeping their communities at arm's length. But too many do, from fear of losing control to the outside world, from the great pressure to fund their organizations, and from trying not to drown in a fast-moving environment.

Working this way is particularly dispiriting and exhausting for executive directors. The result—a dangerously high rate of turnover and burnout for executive directors—has created a widening leadership gap within the sector.

For example, in 2009, the Bridgespan Group reported that more than twenty thousand nonprofit organizations would not have senior leadership for significant periods of time that year. It wasn't that these organizations weren't looking for leaders; rather, they couldn't find people with the skills, passion, and commitment to do jobs that feel increasingly undoable.[5]

In *Working Across Generations*, Frances Kunreuther, Helen Kim, and Robby Rodriguez explain that "the crisis is that the position of executive director as it is currently conceived is no longer viable."[6]

As the Baby Boomers who founded many nonprofit organizations retire from leadership positions, an enormous, idealistic, cause-driven generation—Millennials, or Gen Y—is refusing these overwhelming senior management positions. All organizations need to understand Millennials and their work styles if they are going to survive and thrive in the future.

THE RISE OF MILLENNIALS

Millennials are young people born approximately between the years 1978 and 1992. Most people think the Baby Boomers are the largest living generation, but in fact, there were 77.6 million Millennials compared to 74.1 million Baby Boomers in 2008. They are the most racially diverse generation in American history. According to the Center for Information & Research on Civic Learning & Engagement (CIRCLE) at the University of Maryland, "between 1968 and 2006, the percentage of young residents who are white has fallen from 88 percent in 1968 to 62 percent in 2006. During the same period, the percentage of young people who are African-American or Hispanic has grown by 2.3 and 10.6 percentage points respectively."[7]

In 2008, the Case Foundation commissioned a paper called "Social Citizens[BETA]" that examined the role of Millennials in social change efforts.[8] The paper outlined the unique characteristics of Millennials that shape their outlook on life, define their effect on organizations, and make them invaluable for social change. The paper noted that Millennials have grown up in a society marinating in causes, from their schools and congregations, to MTV, to blogs and Facebook and MySpace. Millennials, like all of us, are asked to raise and give money, sign petitions, and buy environmentally friendly products. It's having an effect: in a 2006 research study, 74 percent of Millennials said they were more likely to buy a product when they felt that the company had a deep commitment to a cause.[9]

Millennials were also the first generation to have volunteerism as a requirement starting in middle school. In 2008, 83 percent of public high schools and 77 percent of middle schools had mandatory community service requirements. According to the Corporation for National and Community Service, teenage volunteerism declined between 1974 and 1989 (20.9 percent and 13.4 percent, respectively), but more than doubled between 1989 and 2005 (from 13.4 percent to 28.4 percent). In addition, the number of volunteering college students increased 20 percent between 2002 and 2005, signifying that they are sustaining volunteerism beyond high school.[10]

And, of course, Millennials are digital natives, born clicking, friending, poking, e-mailing, and texting. They are the first generation of people born with no memory of life without the World Wide Web; they are living connected, digital lives in an entirely new way.

Millennials use MySpace and Facebook as their home base for managing and growing far-flung social networks. These sites are the corner soda shops of their generation. Sixty-five percent of teens use online social networks, compared with 35 percent of adults, although they use them in similar ways—to stay in contact with existing friends, make new friends, and make plans.[11]

The combination of idealism and social media fluency makes Millennials passionate about causes, but not passionate, necessarily, about nonprofit organizations. Because they view the world through the lens of social media and social networks, Millennials are less interested in institutions than their parents were. They don't see walls where others used to because in their world, information sharing and power has shifted toward individuals. This creates a huge distinction in their minds between a cause they're passionate about, such as cancer research, and a stand-alone nonprofit organization they may not care about at all.

If alarm bells aren't ringing inside of nonprofit organizations right now, they should be—loudly.

Millennials represent a potential fatal blow to the large, ongoing membership donor bases for traditional organizations. They are highly unlikely to become lifetime members and donors to groups like their grandparents were. Millennials are more likely to retain their passion for causes and giving in general, and perhaps even particular causes, but also jump from organization to organization as a particular effort moves them.

Millennials' passions are fluid; they will support organizations at certain times when moved to do so, and then they will go away. To adapt and survive, organizations will have to become more flexible and accepting of this reality.

Another issue is that Millennials expect organizations to have the same fluency with social media, the same comfort working beyond the organization's institutional walls as they do. Thus, organizations that don't yet work as networks experience inherent tension and conflict with Millennials. Engaging these seventy million passionate people as staff members but also supporters, fundraisers, friend raisers, and organizers on their behalf is a very important reason for nonprofit organizations to transform themselves into Networked Nonprofits.

Millennials, with their passion for causes and fluency with social media, are also a part of a powerful new force for social change called *free agents*. **Free agents** are individuals working outside of organizations to organize, mobilize, raise funds, and communicate with constituents. In the old paradigm, organizations could dismiss free agents as amateurs not worthy of their time and attention. And without the connectedness of social media they might have been able to afford to ignore them. But not any more, not with the power of an entire social movement in the palm of an individual's hand.

Free agents are not by definition Millennials, but many free agents are young people. Free agents take advantage of the social media toolset to do everything organizations have always done, but outside of institutional walls.

FREE AGENTS IN ACTION

In October 2008, Amanda Rose, a young Canadian marketing executive living in London, and a few friends—Ben Matthews, Tom Malcolm, Renate Nyborg, and Tom Hoang—asked their Twitter followers, at that time the fastest growing social network on the Web, a question. If Facebook was being used to raise money for charities, largely through an **application** called Causes, could Twitter be used to do the same?

The immediate response to the question was "Yes!" The next question was: Which cause? Again, Amanda and her friends engaged their network of friends in a conversation. Should we focus on one cause or a few? How should we raise money for whichever causes we choose? After a series of open conversations on Twitter, they decided to raise money for a nonprofit organization called charity: water, which supports clean water projects in developing countries. charity: water met all of the criteria that their growing group of Twitter followers were interested in—it had global reach, a simple mission, and a staff that were facile and appreciative of social media.

A plan took shape through more conversations on Twitter. Twestival, as the effort became known, would take place on February 12, 2009, with an original goal of 40–50 events across the United States to raise money for charity: water. Amanda was astonished as more and more people volunteered to organize local Twestivals. The effort quickly reached 75 events, and then surpassed 100 with events in places such as England, Germany, Argentina, Japan, and even Africa. Eventually, over the course of just three weeks, Twestival had 202 events scheduled worldwide.

Amanda and charity: water let Twestival become whatever local organizers wanted it to be. Some events were organized as dinners at restaurants, which agreed to discount the food and drinks. Organizers used Twitter to get the word out, but also contacted their local media—including newspapers, television stations, and bloggers—to publicize events. They also asked companies to donate items for auction, hosted cocktail parties and dinner parties, and held raffles.

Beginning in Asia on February 12, Twestival unfolded across the globe, working its way across Europe and Africa, North and South America, and ending in Honolulu at midnight Pacific Time. In the end, Twestival raised over $250,000 for charity: water—at a cost of zero to the organization.[12] Twestival's inaugural effort wasn't its last, as it has continued to spread its reach and fundraising power around the globe. (Figure 2.1 shows the Twestival logo.)

Amanda Rose had become the Bob Geldoff of her generation. Beginning in the 1980s, Geldoff had organized large-scale concerts around the world to raise money for poverty relief. His model reflected the twentieth-century broadcast era that required enormous amounts of capital, celebrity power, and hired staff, technicians, and consultants to be successful.

But Twestival reflected Amanda's outlook as a Millennial, using social media to power decentralized networks of individuals volunteering their time and talent to self-organize small events around the world. Amanda is a very powerful free agent for social change.

Free agent activists are an important, growing part of the social change equation. They are not competition for organizations, but allies, amazing **influencers** who can attract large numbers of new people to support various causes—if they are engaged well.

Many free agents, like Amanda Rose and Peggy Padden, are working on behalf of nonprofit organizations. Others are not connected to any particular organization.

**Figure 2.1
Twestival Logo**

Source: Printed with the permission of Amanda Rose.

In December 2007, ten-year-old Laura Stockman pledged to do twenty-five good deeds leading up to Christmas in memory of her grandfather who had died the previous year. The fifth-grader started a blog, Twenty-Five Days to Make a Difference, to share her ideas and efforts with other people in the hope they might want to do the same.

Her efforts resonated with people, including several influential philanthropic bloggers, and word began to spread across the blogosphere. In addition, the local broadcast news media in her hometown of Buffalo, New York, shared her story. After just her first week of blogging, Laura had 16,000 visitors to her Web site from all around the country and the world, including China, Australia, Africa, and South America.

Laura continued blogging past that first Christmas, engaging in an ongoing conversation with readers about causes they were interested in, projects others might want to join, and volunteering in general. She has helped to raise thousands of dollars for such causes as the ASPCA, and helps get books and clothing donated to shelters.

Some organizations may consider free agents firecrackers—untrained, unsupervised, unpredictable individuals wandering into territory specifically designated for professionals. But dismissing them so quickly would be a huge missed opportunity. Free agents are a fundamental part of the new landscape and an important, exciting component of networked social change. And nonprofit organizations need to work with them, not against them or beside them, going forward.

ORGANIZATIONS WORKING WITH FREE AGENTS

The rise of free agents doesn't diminish the need for nonprofit organizations. They serve as a community's institutional memory, and they support experts who need salaries and funding to accomplish their work. Moreover, organizations are easier to fund than individuals and can create hubs of information and resources. We need nonprofit organizations, but we need them to become different, better, and more effective at engaging supporters and addressing social problems than they have been.

One way in particular that nonprofit organizations have to change is by embracing free agents. Relationships between free agents and nonprofit organizations can be mutually beneficial. Free agents need nonprofit expertise and structure to provide a legal and programmatic infrastructure to their efforts.

Organizations, however, need to be agile and open enough to leverage free agents and their energetic social networks.

Nonprofit organizations are beginning to reach out to free agents. Tyson Foods, in partnership with Share Our Strength, the Capital Area Food Bank of Texas, and leading bloggers like Chris Brogan, sponsored the Pledge to End Hunger. For every thousand people who signed the online pledge form, Tyson donated 34 pounds of Tyson food products to the food bank. Free agents were encouraged to blog about the campaign, sign the pledge themselves, and spread the word in other creative ways. Nearly five thousand pledges were made. [13]

A few rules of engagement exist for working with free agents:

• **Get to know the free agents**. Organizations must prioritize building personal relationships with the key free agents in their network. Free agents may be bloggers or Twitterers, superstar Facebook Causes organizers, or passionate people with large e-mail lists. The tools they use to build and nurture their network are not as important as the influence they wield outside of the organization's walls. Organizations need to get to know who the agents are and what they are passionate about. Read their blogs and e-mails, call them, take them to lunch, find out why they do what they do. Build trust now, and it will be reciprocated in the future.

• **Break out of silos**. The ethnographer danah boyd notes, "We live in homogenous networks, and self-organizing magnifies cliques." [14] Nonprofit organizations need to help people to break out of their cliques, not reinforce them. "Volunteering is certainly widespread and in that sense it is an ethos, but it's an ethos that is also an echo," says Harry Boyte, the founder and codirector of the Institute's Center for Democracy and Citizenship, at the Hubert H. Humphrey Institute of Public Affairs at the University of Minnesota.[15]

• **Young people and free agents need to explore and learn about issues and sort out their feelings about them**. Nonprofit organizations can help to create these places for exploration. Free agents need to challenge the thinking of organizations and advocates without the pressure of conforming to conventional wisdom or any particular agenda.

• **Don't ignore the newcomer**. It may go against the grain of traditional organizational thinking to spend energy cultivating relationships with uncredentialed, perhaps young, newcomers. But ignoring them is a lost opportunity, as you never know who will share their stories and their passion for a cause and move others to action.

Take Drew Olanoff, for example. He was stunned to learn he had cancer at twenty-nine years old. But two of his greatest assets didn't fail him at this critical time: his sense of humor and his facility with social media. Drew created a Web site, **www.blamedrewscancer.com**, and a Twitter page to share his anger and use his humor to help him deal with the diagnosis. He decided to blame his cancer for everyday things, like losing his car keys or a loss by his beloved Phillies.

Word spread about Drew's tongue-in-cheek effort. Eventually, Lance Armstrong weighed in on Twitter that he was blaming Drew's cancer for his sore shoulder. Drew then guest-blogged at LIVESTRONG where readers were encouraged to donate a dollar per complaint. Lance and LIVESTRONG understood that it was important to embrace Drew and his network of supporters.

• **Keep the welcome sign lit**. Even if a free agent is passionately involved with an organization for a period of time, it does not mean that he or she will be in the future. That's why they're free agents! They come and go at their discretion, not at the organization's behest. Still, keep the doors open for them to return whenever they want with their large networks and good energy in tow.

• **Let them go**. Free agents may not do what organizations want them to do, but that doesn't mean they aren't participating and helping. For instance, instead of donating, they might take out their megaphone and ask their networks to participate and give. They could also provide or leverage in-kind donations and help organize events. Organizations need to let free agents participate when and how they want.

• **Don't be afraid to follow**. It can be difficult for professional staff to admit they didn't come up with a great idea. But worrying about who came up with what idea is a waste of energy. Ideas don't have to be born within institutional walls to be good. Organizations need to listen for the great ideas that are out there, leverage them (or just parts of them), and embrace their originators without needing to "own" either the free agent or the idea.

We are just beginning to see the myriad ways people can use the social web to share their passion for their favorite causes. Free agents are a huge, largely untapped resource for nonprofit organizations. With a little understanding, encouragement, and strategic thinking, organizations and free agents will become remarkable resources for one another.

CONCLUSION

The need to change the way that nonprofit organizations are structured and operate cannot be ignored. Social media provides one kind of urgent incentive to change and embrace the new tools and rhythms of working in connected ways. But the crisis of leadership and structure of nonprofit organizations, the rise of Millennials and free agents, cannot be ignored or dismissed. They highlight the need for nonprofits to embrace a new way of thinking and working as networks. We begin our journey of transformation by exploring all the elements—functioning as social networks, simplifying work, becoming transparent, and building external relationships—that make Networked Nonprofits so effective.

PART ONE How to Become a Networked Nonprofit

Everyone thinks about changing the world,
but no one thinks of changing himself.

—Leo Tolstoy

Understanding Social Networks

Networked Nonprofits shift their focus from working as single organizations to working as part of larger social networks that exist inside and outside of their institutional walls. This enables Networked Nonprofits to transform an idea or grievance into an army of passionate supporters for social change in an instant.

Traditionally, organizations have viewed themselves through an organization-centric lens. Envisioning oneself and one's organization as the center of the universe with other people and organizations circling around it—providing it with funds, attention, and volunteers as needed—is at odds with a world energized by social media and connectedness. Other organizations and individuals are not waiting for instructions for what to do; they're talking, doing, and connecting based on their own needs and interests. Networked Nonprofits know this and are reorienting themselves to engage with individual free agents and organizations in their networks.

Organizations don't have to create these social networks; they exist all around us in a variety of forms. Networked Nonprofits strengthen and expand these networks by building relationships within them to engage and activate them for their organizations' efforts. Networked Nonprofits also know how to identify, reach, and cultivate the influencers within their social networks, which is the key to growing very big quickly and inexpensively.

Social networks come in many shapes and sizes. In this book, we will focus on

- Personal social networks that include family and friends, neighborhood members, fellow congregants, and hobbyists.
- Professional networks of colleagues within organizations, plus people who work at collegial agencies, funders, government agencies, associations, and more.

25

- Self-organized networks of individuals on sites such as Facebook where people voluntarily "friend" one another.
- Networks of people created by specific nonprofit organizations. This means, in essence, pulling members out of their databases and connecting them to one another through online social networks that organizations like charity: water are hosting on their Web sites.

Networked Nonprofits work effectively with any combination of these networks. We call this combination of social networks filled with individuals and organizations an organization's ecosystem.

In this chapter, we will explain what social networks are and how they operate. We will define the components of social networks and describe how to map them in order to identify ways to grow and strengthen them. Finally, we will examine how organizations can weave these networks to create social change.

THE CHANGING CONTEXT OF SOCIAL NETWORKS

Nature is rife with examples of work and life organized to benefit a whole group. Hives, herds, and packs enable bees, buffalo, and coyotes to organize and protect themselves for the benefit of individual members and the entire group. Human beings organized themselves similarly; we used to call them tribes. Now we call them social networks.

In the last half of the twentieth century, the nature of these networks began to change. We became a mobile society, moving to the far corners of the country and the earth in increasingly large numbers. This mobility was particularly noticeable in job tenures that shortened over the last several decades. According to the U.S. Department of Labor, workers in almost every age group are staying at their jobs for shorter periods of time than their counterparts did in the 1980s. For instance, in 2008 twenty-five- to thirty-four-year-olds held their current jobs for a median of 2.7 years, down from three years in 1983.[1] The devastating effect that mobility had on communities was dramatically captured by Robert Putnam in his book *Bowling Alone*, published in 2000. Unmoored from extended families and communities, working longer hours, mesmerized by in-home entertainment, we had turned into a nation of couch potatoes, sitting at home, alone.

Near the end of the century, this trend started to reverse itself. Social media tools such as e-mail and online social networks such as Facebook and

MySpace began to connect millions of people to one another and reformulate neighborhoods online. These new networks became places to virtually wave to a neighbor on the corner or catch up on the latest news at the grocery store. Online communities are not a substitute for in-person connections, and they never will be, but they do serve an important purpose in keeping us connected to old friends and enabling us to meet new ones.

Indeed, these networks are more than random gatherings of people online. Social networks have specific structures and patterns to them. In order to engage them well, organizations need to understand the fundamental building blocks of social networks.

UNDERSTANDING SOCIAL NETWORKS

At their most basic level, social networks are simple, intuitive structures. They have two main components: people or organizations called **nodes** (in network speak) and the connections between them called **ties**. The nodes are important, of course, but without the ties the network doesn't exist. For example, toddlers engaged in parallel play are like network nodes without the ties. These children are physically around other people, but are essentially playing alone.

Hubs are the larger nodes within networks, meaning the people or organizations that have lots of connections. Hubs are the influencers in the network, the people who know everyone and are known by everyone. They enjoy sharing information and connecting people to one another and resources.

Of course, hubs existed before social media. In her seminal book on urban planning, *The Death and Life of Great American Cities*, Jane Jacobs described hubs in her neighborhood in the late 1950s this way: "The social structure of sidewalk life hangs partly on what can be called self-appointed public characters. A public character is anyone who is in frequent contact with a wide circle of people and who is sufficiently interested to make himself a public character. His main qualification is that he is public, that he talks to lots of different people. In this way, news travels that is of sidewalk interest." [2]

Hubs make things go "viral" online. Going viral happens when huge numbers of people have watched a video or read a blog post or clicked on something. Word may start to spread friend-to-friend, but the tipping point generally occurs when a hub shares the news. Jake Brewer, the former Internet manager at the Energy Action Coalition, described his organization's efforts to cultivate hubs in their network to work on their behalf this way: "If we get one thousand video views that is good. The comments are a focus group with our influencers. If they like it, they'll spread it all over YouTube."[3] Reaching and engaging the hubs as Brewer's organization did is the most efficient and least expensive way to spread news and ideas, raise awareness, and activate people to do something for a cause.

Hub status does not happen because of a person's position on an organizational chart. Anyone within an organization, regardless of his or her position, can become a hub as a blogger or a Twitter user. Free agents can also be hubs in a network. Influential individual bloggers such as David Armano and Chris Brogan send their readers to various places on the Web to read blog posts, view videos, and start conversations for and against companies and causes. Armano describes his network as an online neighborhood where people know and care about one another.

Networks also have cores. The **core** is the inner cluster of people who do most of the work on any project or effort. Clay Shirky describes this dynamic in *Here Comes Everybody*: "Fewer than 2 percent of Wikipedia users ever contribute, yet it is enough to create profound value for millions of users." This imbalance, called the **power law of distribution**, applies to most areas of the social Web. A small handful of blogs get the most traffic, and a small number of Twitter users have the largest number of followers.[4]

Clusters are groups of people who are connected to one another, but who have few connections to the rest of the network. Clusters occur in organizations that tend toward silos. Clusters are often isolated from the other parts of the network, and intentional efforts need to be made to connect them to the rest of the network.

The network structures discussed so far are intuitive and understandable given our life experiences within social networks. However, two additional characteristics of networks are counterintuitive but essential to networks' effectiveness.

First, the network's **edge or periphery** is vital to its growth. Traditional hierarchical organizations wouldn't spend much time paying attention to the periphery because it doesn't appear to have as much power or influence in the network as the core or the hubs. Yet people in the periphery are important because they are likely to be participants, perhaps even the core or hubs, in other networks. They can help the network grow by connecting it with other networks, and they can bring new people, energy, and ideas into a network. In this way, the periphery plays a critical role in the elasticity of networks, and enables them to grow and expand rapidly.

The second counterintuitive notion about social networks is that effective networks are made up not only of strong ties between nodes, but of a combination of strong and loose ties. Strong ties are the relationships you have with close personal friends or relatives. Loose ties are lighter connections that friendly acquaintances have with one another. These light ties can become powerfully activated for a cause.

An example of activating lighter ties for a cause was the presidential campaign of Barack Obama. Supporters reached out through their personal social networks using e-mail and Facebook and encouraged everyone they knew to support their candidate. They didn't just select people they knew to be politically engaged, they reached out to everyone, including second cousins and third-grade classmates. And it worked. Obama supporters were often people who had never been politically active before. They were moved to support his candidacy for a wide variety of reasons, but an especially effective mechanism was being asked by friends and family to do so.

Social media are remarkably powerful tools for nurturing loose ties over time. Blogger Leisa Reichelt describes this as social media's ability to create ambient intimacy. She wrote, "Ambient intimacy is about being able to keep in touch with people with a level of regularity and intimacy that you wouldn't usually have access to because time and space conspire against it."[5]

Loose ties are created online every day when grade-school friends reconnect on Facebook. This would have taken a tremendous amount of work to achieve in the analog world. The power of ambient intimacy is that once the ties are established online, they are easy to maintain. It just takes an occasional e-mail or Facebook post to share family news, ask advice, or simply to touch base. In this way, ambient intimacy makes social networks geometrically larger than they would be on land.

Overall, networks made up entirely of strong ties don't expand; they are tight-knit cliques. Networks made up only of loose ties are too weak to get anything done. Social networks made of a combination of loose and strong ties can move information through the network quickly and effectively as they grow and add new people.

Now that we know the components of social networks—the nodes, ties, hubs, and periphery—it is important to "see" a network to understand how it works and how it can be strengthened and expanded. We need to map the network in order to see it.

MAPPING AN ORGANIZATION'S SOCIAL NETWORK

Social **network mapping** tools run the gamut from simple to complex, free to expensive, and low-tech to high-tech (see the sidebar for a list of examples). High-end social network analysis software can generate dazzling pictures that yield myriad interesting data and insights about who is connected to whom.

But don't be dismayed if your organization can't afford these tools—you can still map your network. One is a method for mapping an organization's ecosystem by hand. The other uses free online tools to map a social network on one particular social media channel like Facebook or Twitter. We will describe both processes below.

The hand-drawn network mapping and analysis discussed here is based on the terrific, low-tech process developed by Eva Schiffer while she worked in Africa on a project funded by the International Food Policy Research Institute and CGAIR Challenge Program on Food and Water.[6] We have modified Eva's process based on our own experiences and the context of mapping social networks for domestic nonprofit organizations. The only things that the mappers will need for this process are a willingness to engage, a flip chart, a handful of different colored markers, and different colored sticky notes.

As an example, we will draw the social network of a hypothetical organization called The Kids' Book Club. The Kids' Book Club is a nonprofit organization that donates free books for children living in homeless shelters. Volunteers gather donated books and deliver them to the shelters as gifts for the children. Though it seems simple, this effort requires an array of individuals and organizations working in concert to be successful and sustainable.

Key individuals and organizations are asked to participate in the mapping process. For the Kids' Book Club this means staff, volunteers, shelter personnel, and donors. They begin by discussing what they hope to learn from the mapping process and what problems mapping the network will solve. The Kids' Book Club wants to find out who the hubs are in their network and who is at the periphery in order to better engage more and different types of people in their efforts.

The group then brainstorms about the nodes in the network. Who are the key people and organizations that should be included on their map? Do they provide information, services, or funding? Each type of node is assigned a different colored sticky note. The Kids' Book Club nodes include the people in the room, plus the county social services agency, book publishers who donate some books in bulk, and the public library.

The nodes are written down on the sticky notes and placed on the flip chart. Lines connect the nodes to one another. The sticky notes may need to be maneuvered as the lines begin to become complicated. The group discusses how the nodes are connected, whether formal or informal arrangements exist between them, and whether the relationship is one way (with an arrow pointed in that direction) or two ways (with the arrow pointed in both directions). They also indicate the strength of the relationships: a thicker line for stronger ties, thinner line, or dots for loose ties. Once this is completed, the Kids' Book Club has a basic network map that visually illustrates who is connected to whom—and how—in their ecosystem.

What could the Kids' Book Club learn from this exercise?

They may learn that the network hubs are the homeless shelters rather than the organization. This confirms what they all suspected—that the shelters, not the organization, really drive the program. This may also be fine with everyone, but it's good to know for certain to help organize and manage the effort moving forward.

The map is also useful for illustrating who is missing from the ecosystem. The two groups who most influence children may not be on the map: parents and schools. That finding could begin a conversation about why they aren't on the map and how they could be invited to participate more in the program.

Of course, organizations are engaged with more than one social network in their efforts. To that end, organizations can also map online social networks developed through the use of tools like Twitter and Facebook for greater understanding and insight. To illustrate how this is done, we will use a real-life example of an organization mapping their social network on Twitter.

Wildlife Watch is a program of the National Wildlife Federation. The goal of the program is to encourage people to appreciate wildlife and wildlife conservation and share their observations with others in an online database. Jessica Jones manages the program. Part of her effort involves engaging people on Twitter to listen and tell stories about the efforts of individuals (she calls them citizen scientists) to participate in cataloging the natural world around them. As of this writing, she had a Twitter following of 1,565 people.

Jessica wanted to know who the influencers were on her Twitter network. She decided to use a free social network analysis tool called Mailana to analyze her Twitter community.[7]

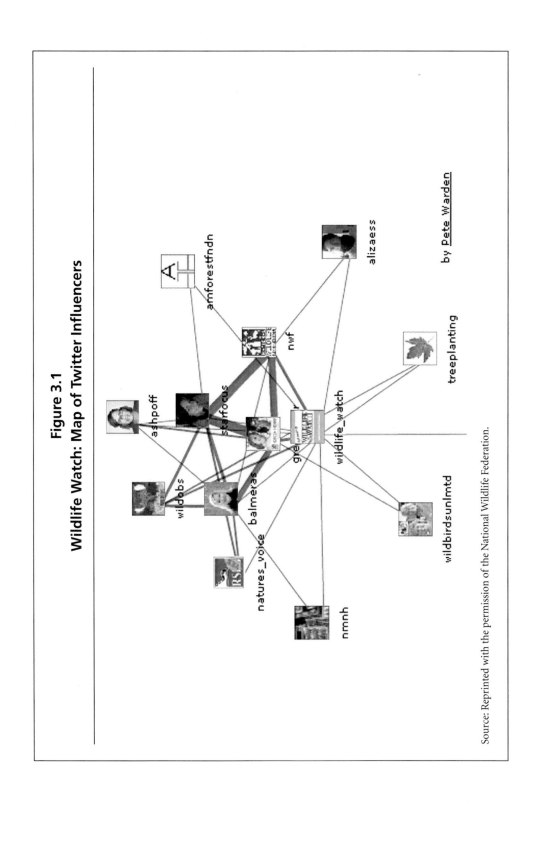

Figure 3.1
Wildlife Watch: Map of Twitter Influencers

by Pete Warden

amforestfndn

nwf

alizaess

treeplanting

ashpoff

stalfocus

wildobs

greer

wildlife_watch

balmeras

wildbirdsunlmtd

natures_voice

nmnh

Source: Reprinted with the permission of the National Wildlife Federation.

The map in Figure 3.1 shows that Jessica's network has about a half-dozen "influencers" or hubs. These individuals or organizations have forwarded or "retweeted" the largest number of Jessica's messages.

These hubs have a few interesting characteristics. First, they are all closely connected to one another, except for the one on the periphery. Second, there is a difference in the size of the lines between the Wildlife Program and these six influencers. Mapping the hubs enables Jessica to focus her energies on building her relationship with them. The one hub at the periphery isn't an outcast but an opportunity to build relationships with a more distant network.

These two examples show how useful network mapping is for understanding social networks and improving their effectiveness for organizations. But knowing what a network looks like is one thing; being able to use it for social change is another. The question that organizations need to ask and answer is: How do you activate the people in these social networks to do something on behalf of our organization and causes?

THE NOT-SO-SECRET NETWORK SAUCE: SOCIAL CAPITAL

We know from our own personal experiences that some social networks, say an alumni network or a congregation, are very energetic and active. In these networks, information and resources are shared easily and freely, and people enjoy and benefit from their participation. Conversely, other social networks are listless. Nothing happens in these networks, no one shares or does anything, and they don't seem to have any energy or drive. What's the difference between these networks? The first has a lot of the not-so-secret sauce—**social capital**—and the second one doesn't.

Social capital is the stuff that makes relationships meaningful and resilient. Within such relationships two things generally exist: trust and reciprocity. People do things for one another because they trust that their motives are good and that they will receive something in return some time in the future. When a person drops everything late at night to help a friend change a tire, trust and reciprocity exist. When someone donates twenty dollars to a cause that may not interest her but is her brother's passion, she does so because of social capital.

Social media builds social capital. In particular, online social networks are filled with it. That's why people are connected to one another. And organizations need to build, nurture, strengthen, and use this capital for social change to occur.

Let's compare a scenario with a dearth of social capital to one bubbling over with it.

Imagine that you receive an e-mail from someone named joesmith@children .com with the subject line: *Save the Kids!* The e-mail contains a photo of a child sitting in a classroom in your town without any books or school supplies. The e-mail asks you to forward the photo to ten neighbors and to consider donating to your local school foundation. You don't know Joe, you don't have any kids in the local schools, you just gave to a cause last week that is special to you, you're very busy, and ten more e-mails are in your inbox to read. You are likely to delete this e-mail right away.

Now imagine that your next-door neighbor, Grace, the head of the local PTA, sends you an e-mail with the same subject line, *Save the Kids!*, but from her personal e-mail account. You open it because you know Grace and trust her. You also know that she will ask you about it when you see her walking her dog later today. In addition, you were thinking of asking her if she would bring her special Asian chicken salad to the potluck dinner at church next Sunday, so it would be nice to have already done something special for her. You read the e-mail, send a check for $10 to the school fund, and then forward the e-mail to a few friends.

Your relationship with Grace is full of social capital because of the interactions that you have had with her for years. Social media can create and sustain relationships online that are equally full of social capital.

It is as important to recognize when social capital doesn't exist as when it does. For instance, people can forge relationships during a particularly intense experience, say, during the first year of college or on the first week of a new job. But when the experience fades, so does the relationship. That friendship did not contain any social capital; it was simply a product of those particular circumstances.

Similarly, organizations may think that they have more social capital than they do. For instance, Dave gave money for cancer research in response to a request from his friend Fred. Dave is strongly connected to Fred, but only lightly connected to the cancer research organization. The organization begins to send direct mail fundraising appeals to Dave, which he ignores because he and the organization have no social capital together. Dave *could* become connected to the organization, but only if the organization reaches out and builds stronger ties directly with him. If the organization confuses Dave's check with his capital, then the relationship is doomed.

Social media builds social capital because

- **People are easy to find online and on many channels.** It is easy for individuals to find one another online without intermediaries, brokers, or organizations getting in the way. It is also easy for organizations to find people because what they do and believe and care about is visible.

- **Talk is cheap.** Having conversations is inexpensive online, unburdened by the constraints of mobile minutes and snail-mail stamps. Without these barriers, people and organizations can have multiple conversations at no increase in cost. In addition to words and thoughts, people can share photographs and videos online for free. Social media users can forward the messages of organizations to their networks at no additional cost to the organization. As a result, the cost to scale online efforts can be negligible for organizations.

- **Serendipity is enhanced online.** People can find one another, organizations, and causes online without needing any formal introductions. They can simply bump into one another or search for one another, and develop unexpected and powerful relationships.

- **Reciprocity is incredibly easy.** On-land reciprocity can take time and effort. You may need to buy a card and a stamp, or bake something in return, or remember to call at a decent hour to thank someone. Reciprocity online is incredibly easy and inexpensive. Sending a thank-you e-mail can be done for free in seconds. Posting a thank-you note on Facebook for your community to see is just as easy and even more powerful because it's public. The same can be said of linking to someone on a blog, forwarding a Twitter message, or posting a list of donors on a Web site. Thanking people generously and publicly is an incredibly powerful and easy way to generate social capital online.

Social media is one mechanism for doing all of these things. Still, someone, somewhere, has to actually do them. That someone sends a video link to a key influencer who helps make it go viral, comments on a blog to strengthen the relationship with that blogger, and provides bite-size tasks to the network to enable many people to develop an idea or activity together. That someone is a network weaver.

WEAVING THE NETWORK FOR SOCIAL CHANGE

Network weaving is a term coined by Valdis Krebs and June Holley.[8] It describes a set of skills that help strengthen and build social networks. These online efforts mirror the kinds of engagement, relationship building, and facilitation skills that are crucial elements of community organizing on land.

The efforts of nonprofit social media strategists who are expert network weavers are highlighted throughout this book. Some such as Wendy Harman of the Red Cross, Carie Lewis of the Humane Society, Tom Subak of Planned Parenthood, and Jake Brewer of the Sunlight Foundation work within organizations. Free agents such as Peggy Paddon and Amanda Rose weave their networks from the outside of organizations. Many of these nonprofit practitioners are facile with social media, but as we know from Peggy's experience, this is not a prerequisite to becoming a great network weaver. Rather, continuously learning new ways to use social media to weave a network is a requirement. Weavers energize their networks not just by doing, but by spending considerable time teaching their colleagues, friends, and neighbors how to weave the network as well.

Network weaving activities include

- Introducing and connecting people to one another.
- Facilitating authentic conversations that are meaningful to participants. Sometimes these conversations are actionable, and other times they are simply to build relationships.
- Sharing resources, links, and information without any expectation of a direct return from that person.
- Building relationships with network members by doing things like linking to their blog posts and commenting on blogs, friending them on online social networks, and celebrating their contributions.
- Working with many different people on multiple channels such as e-mail, Facebook, Twitter, blogs, and even on land at face-to-face meetings.
- Treating all members of the network as equals regardless of their formal organizational position.
- Inviting people with differing points of view into conversations, and facilitating those conversations so those points of view can be shared.

Network weavers provide reasons for people to care about causes and organizations. They shape conversations and identify specific ways for people to help. They inspire people to share a message or idea, donate money, and pass legislation that ultimately makes social change happen.

Network weavers don't have to be extroverts or the lives-of-the-party. Craig Newmark, the founder of Craigslist, is a shy person, but he uses social media like a maestro to connect people to one another, share information, and coordinate efforts. Network weavers also don't have to hold any particular position within an organization. Larger organizations may have staff people dedicated to strengthening the organization's presence using social media. However, they are not the only weavers for their organizations. Everyone has the ability to engage with people outside their walls using social media.

Network weaving is a critically important aspect of effective social media usage. When we describe the specific ways that organizations can use social media to advance their efforts—such as working with large numbers of people on a joint project, fundraising, or governance—weaving the network becomes of paramount importance to organizational success.

CONCLUSION

Shifting focus from your organization's workings to the social networks that exist inside and outside of it is a vital and important step in engaging those networks for social change. The networks are filled with people and organizations who want to help. Organizations need to stoke the social capital that exists and weave the network to put them into action. And when they do, wonderful things can happen.

Network Mapping Action Steps

- Identify a mapping team.
- Identify the mapping process that works best for your needs.
- Map your ecosystem.
- Facilitate a conversation with your team. Here are some questions (use mapping questions).
- Determine whether or how network weaving is happening in your organization's network.
- Set up a training to do network weaving.

Organizational Mapping Techniques

Network mapping can take many forms. We share a few descriptions here based on Steve Waddell's work on strategic mapping in "Visual Diagnostics for Mapping and Scaling Change."

Web Crawls: This approach maps and analyzes relationships between URLs, giving a picture of how organizations and issues are connected virtually that is increasingly important in any strategy. Because URLs are usually associated with organizations, crawls quickly identify organizations working in a particular issue system.

Web Scrapes: Web scrapes use either manual or automated qualitative analysis of text on Web sites. The purpose is to identify the usage of key words and phrases, as well as who is using which ones.

Social/Organizational/Inter-Organizational Network Analysis (SNA/ONA/IONA): This is classic social network analysis applied specifically to understanding relationships within and between organizations. These approaches describe the existence and relative importance of relationships between individuals and organizations.

Conceptual Mapping: Often in complex arenas, particular conceptual lenses or "cuts" on the issue bring fresh insights into activities and relationships. Examples include looking at relationship types in terms of organizational sector or seeing how activities play out when considered as different stages or phases. There are various ways of succinctly mapping these, depending on the question.

Mind Mapping: This technique represents the relationship between a central concept and related words, ideas, or tasks. This supports planning, problem solving, and decision making.

Source: Steve Waddell, "Visual Diagnostics for Mapping and Scaling Change,"**http://www .scalingimpact.net/content/strategic-mapping-and-visual-diagnostics-scaling-change** (accessed on January 12, 2010).

REFLECTION QUESTIONS

- What organizations work in the ecosystem for your social change issue? Do they have a presence on Facebook, Twitter, or other social networks? Who are your potential collaborators?

- Are you connected or not connected to these organizations? Draw lines. Identify the hubs and clusters. Where are the loose ties? What are the relationships between your organization or concepts in this system? What influences which aspects or players in this system?

- What are the different roles in your ecosystem?

- What is the relationship between competing and complementary ideas and core concepts? How can you use these relationships to better refine messages and develop synergies?

- If your organization has an organizational presence on Facebook, Twitter, or other networks, what does it look like? How many friends or followers does it have? Who are the influencers or hubs?

- Are the staff members or board members on LinkedIn? Take a look at your collective rolodexes on LinkedIn. Are there influencers or important nodes in these networks whom you need to cultivate and build relationships with to get the work done?

- Think about the touch points you have with people in your network, or that your staff has with people in their network. Are you connecting only to ask for money or give a call to action? Think about reciprocity; what have you given to people in your network before they have asked? How are you appreciating, thanking, and celebrating important people in your online network?

Creating a Social Culture

Hurricane Katrina left a wake of disruption and dismay in its path. One organization that faced significant criticism for its slow response to the hurricane was the American Red Cross. Unfortunately, it didn't hear the criticism swirling around the blogosphere because it wasn't listening. The problem wasn't that the organization didn't care about the criticism—rather, it didn't have the capacity to listen and track, much less engage with, its critics online.

In response, the American Red Cross initiated its social media strategy. It hired Wendy Harman as a social media integrator to "combat" bloggers and to increase organizational **transparency.** "It felt like we were going to war," says Wendy, whose current title is social media manager. "There were concerns about negative comments—fear even."

Wendy and her colleagues started an online listening effort. Their goals: to correct misinformation, be informed about public opinion, track conversation trends, identify influencers, and build relationships. Wendy recalls, "We needed to listen and engage first before we could do anything successfully with social media." To the surprise of everyone at the American Red Cross—including Wendy—the majority of the conversations they initially heard were positive.

What began as a listening experiment, initially with bloggers and then on Twitter, catalyzed both increased internal adoption of social media and also a shift in the organization's relationships with the world. For example, the organization had previously blocked access to social networking sites such as Facebook from work for security reasons. But in December 2008, fundraising staff worked with the organizations' friends on Facebook to win a $50,000 donation from the Western Union Foundation. Based on this experience, senior staff recognized the opportunities that Facebook presented and granted employees access to it.[1]

41

Outside its walls, the American Red Cross now views negative comments as an opportunity to engage in conversations with the critics, educate them and the broader public about an issue, and improve what they are doing.

Indeed, social media use and listening have become a part of developing programs. In one case, Wendy read a blog post complaining about a Red Cross class at a local affiliate. She forwarded it to the local chapter director, who contacted the blogger directly.

The blogger described what happened next: "Someone found my blog post and told the local chapter director. He called me to talk about it honestly. They care about me and they're willing to go the extra mile. This gives the American Red Cross *huge* points. I am now significantly more likely to take another class than I was before."

As social media use by the staff was increasing, it became clear to Wendy and her colleagues that developing a **social media policy** handbook could help guide staff and expand social media use even further. The policy manual—drafted and approved in 2009—encourages staff, chapters, and volunteers to participate in social media as ambassadors for the Red Cross, without being too prescriptive or restrictive in its use. (See Figure 4.1.)

"Open," "candid," and "listening" are now words associated with the American Red Cross, thanks to a social media strategy that went beyond mere rules and tools for the staff. A fundamental reorientation of the organization occurred that affected the roles of all staffers and improved their engagement with the public. The organization had the beginnings of a **social culture.**

The shift to a social culture is not easy for organizations to make. It requires organizational leaders to practice using social media personally. This use then seeps into organizations, creating institutions that work more openly and inclusively in less-punitive environments.

Organizational culture comes from melding the psychology, attitudes, experiences, and beliefs of the people who lead organizations. Others inside and outside of the organization react to those patterns and norms. The predominant organizational culture affects how staff works individually and in concert, and informs and shapes how the organization intersects with the rest of the world.

Many organizations and staff people consider themselves social. They are friendly and outgoing, host events, and thank donors regularly. In this book, we use the term "social" differently. We use it to mean the power of social media to change relationships among people inside and outside of an organization.

This "social-ness" reflects more than individual habits; it refers to organizations such as the American Red Cross that work differently from traditional organizations in fundamental ways.

Working socially challenges deep-set organizational assumptions about leadership, roles, and structure. It forces organizations to think hard about what's important to manage and what can be left uncontrolled. Social culture strikes at the heart of what organizations value and how they operate.

Organizations with social cultures

- Use social media to engage in two-way conversations about the work of the organization with people inside and outside of the organization

- Embrace mistakes and take calculated risks

- Reward learning and reflection

- Use a "try it and fix it as we go" approach that emphasizes failing fast

- Overcome organizational inertia ("We've always done it this way") through open and robust discussions

- Understand and appreciate that informality and individuality do not indicate a lack of caring, professionalism, or quality

- Trust staff to make decisions and respond rapidly to situations, rather than crawl through endless check-off and approval processes

The Monitor Institute calls the organizational shift to a social culture *working wikily*.[2] This is a play on the term ***wiki***, an online workspace for people and organizations to collaborate on ideas and strategies. The shift to working wikily is shown in Figure 4.2.

Another way of describing a social culture comes from blogger Geoff Livingston, who calls the transition to a social culture one that moves from silos to hives: "A hive architecture allows for fluid information transfer and interaction between roles, as well as more open access to the outside."[3]

Organizations with social cultures spend a lot of time talking with people outside of the organization through a variety of social media channels. These are real conversations intended to persuade people to behave or act in certain ways, not window dressing with an ulterior motive.

Everyone in the organization—not just one department—is engaged in these conversations. When the talking begins, people begin to bump into one another

Figure 4.1

Red Cross Social Media Policy and Operations Handbook

---

wharman

| | Search this site |

Social Media Strategy Handbook

CrossnetToolkit2009.7.16

Social Media Handbook for Local Red Cross Units

Introduction I Complete Handbook PDF [link to attached document titled 2009.7.16SocialMediaHandbook.doc] I Handbook Powerpoint [embed attached ppt titled Social Media Handbook] I FAQ I Contact

Social Media Handbook
Listen I Learn I Participate I Create I Implement

Social MediaTools
Blogging I Facebook Page I Facebook Cause I Flickr I YouTube I Twitter

Introduction

This handbook is meant for all Red Crossers interested in how social media can help us deliver our mission critical services.

This information will **familiarize you** with our national social media philosophy, **invite**

American Red Cross Personal Online Communications Guidelines

American Red Cross Online Communications Guidelines

CORPORATE COMMUNICATIONS

If your unit is planning to utilize social media tools to convey a message or augment a communication campaign, Communication and Marketing can advise you in developing a Web 2.0 strategy.

Please review the Online Communications Guidelines for personal communications and contact Wendy Harman at (202) 303-4080 or at HarmanW@usa.redcross.org:

1. For assistance in launching your campaigndeveloping a social media strategy for your chapter or blood region.
2. To notify national headquarters about your official online activities.

PERSONAL COMMUNICATIONS

Figure 4.1
Red Cross Social Media Policy and Operations Handbook
(*Continued*)

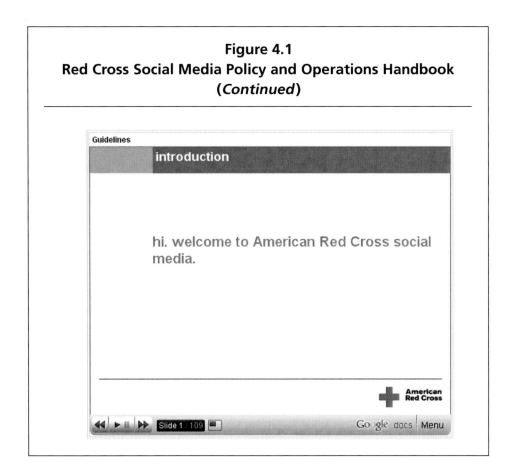

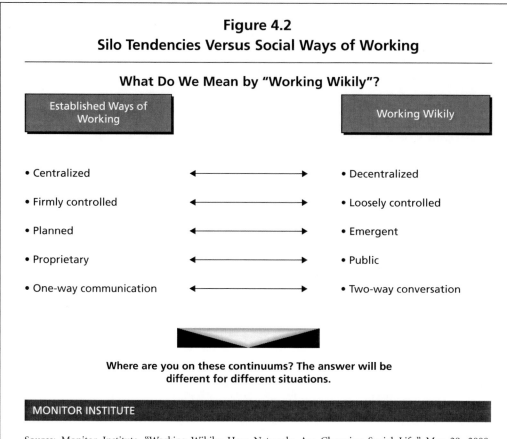

Figure 4.2
Silo Tendencies Versus Social Ways of Working

What Do We Mean by "Working Wikily"?

Established Ways of Working		Working Wikily
• Centralized	⟷	• Decentralized
• Firmly controlled	⟷	• Loosely controlled
• Planned	⟷	• Emergent
• Proprietary	⟷	• Public
• One-way communication	⟷	• Two-way conversation

Where are you on these continuums? The answer will be different for different situations.

MONITOR INSTITUTE

Source: Monitor Institute, "Working Wikily: How Networks Are Changing Social Life," May 29, 2008, **http://workingwikily.net/?page_id=149** (accessed on May 23, 2009). Reprinted with the permission of the Monitor Institute.

not just at the end of the hallway or around the water cooler, but on Facebook and Twitter, too. These casual interactions enable people to learn and share experiences and ideas, and talk about the work and the organization. The result: unique, innovative ideas that may come from new and unusual contributors.

Organizations without social cultures may grudgingly give approval for junior staffers or interns to start using social media tools. These organizations may create a Facebook page or a blog, and they may even get some traction with these efforts. However, over time these efforts will fade because the oxygen needed for them to thrive—authentic conversation—requires leadership's attention and appreciation to exist.

With or without the knowledge or approval of organizational leaders, social behavior is beginning to happen within almost every organization. Staffers are sharing information about their organizations with their friends through forwarded e-mails and personal Facebook page posts many people can see. Bloggers are writing about organizations, and the commenters on these blogs continue the discussion.

Organizations cannot stop this from happening—and they shouldn't try to. Sharing information and connecting with people outside of organizations comes naturally, more so with the power of social media in everyone's hands.

That said, stealth adoption from the bottom up will only work well for a little while and for smaller efforts. Organizational culture won't change without the buy-in and support of organizational leaders.

CHANGE IS HARD

Our friend Sam told us this story about his frustration working in a hierarchical organization that wasn't ready to embrace a social culture:

> I am a nonprofit development professional. I'm comfortable using social networks and other social media sites. Although I use them as an individual, I see great potential for my nonprofit organization's fundraising efforts.
>
> Not long ago, I created a minor stir by advocating that our voluntary young professionals group (host of several fundraising events and a responsibility in my job description) immediately start using Facebook, including the step of inviting current institution members to join a Facebook group. I was asked by marketing to submit a full proposal to them about Facebook and get their approval before going forward and for anything I post to the group.
>
> The young professionals group revolted. They are now using Facebook on their own. They recently agreed to add me as an administrator for the group.
>
> This could have been avoided if we could just have the conversation across departments about our policy and approach to social network sites—from what we can do personally/individually to how we'll support, facilitate, or work with self-forming groups on social networks that want to support our institution. My offer to help

kick-start, research, and join the social networking policy development process at work (from a fundraiser perspective) was also rebuffed.

Why is our institution stuck in silos, and how can we transition out of this so we can effectively deploy a social networking strategy across boundaries of departments?[4]

Sam's experience illustrates that bad things happen to organizations that bring their old, proprietary behaviors online. His organization isn't going to change until the leadership thinks differently about social media, and is open to having conversations with staff about its use. Indeed, organizations trying to use social media without a social culture will be very lonely online. They will miss the robust, roiling conversation happening out there, in cyberspace, about their issues and organization simply because they're not listening or participating.

While some organizations will not be able to make the shift to being social because they are stuck in time, others are Brundleflies. Remember the 1986 movie *The Fly*? The lead character Seth Brundle, played by Jeff Goldblum, accidentally merges himself with a housefly and becomes a grotesque hybrid creation he calls a Brundlefly. He lives a brief, tortured existence in a suspended state of transition. So it is with organizations that start transitions but never finish them, trapping themselves in a purgatory of enervating disappointment. These organizations are Brundleflies.

In 2007, the Overbrook Foundation surveyed seventy-five human rights grantees to assess their social media use. Half these grantees reported having blogs. But only half of those, a quarter of the total grantees surveyed, allowed comments. These organizations assumed that by opening themselves up to comments they would automatically receive a flood of criticism and complaints for the world to see, including their funders and board members.[5] These organizations were Brundleflies, halfway between siloed organizations and social ones, locked in old organizational cultures of fear.

Whether a nonprofit organization refuses to change or is stuck in transition, however, the reality is that organizations have no choice but to change. The alternative is to be left behind in a more open and social world. Organizations that have slipped into the habit of spending enormous amounts of time thinking and worrying about everything that could go wrong will find this shift particularly challenging.

Yes, something could go wrong, but much more is likely to go right when an organization opens itself up. And though new users may fear criticism, the bigger threat to the organization is the deafening silence that happens when organizations are antisocial and isolated from their communities. As Wendy Harman of the Red Cross says, "Silence is indifference, and that is worse than negative comments."[6]

Thus, the first step for organizational leaders in becoming more social is to face, and hopefully overcome, their fears of what could possibly go wrong if they open themselves up personally and professionally by using social media.

WHAT WE FEAR MOST IS . . .

The fears that newcomers have of using social media and opening themselves up are real and understandable. They strike at the heart of what so many organizational leaders were taught was their job: to protect their organizations from harm by controlling everything that happens inside and outside of their walls. Bill Traynor calls this fear of losing control "vertigo." He writes:

> Vertigo is a state caused by being out of balance in relation to your environment. Moving from a traditional environment to a network or connected environment can cause a kind of vertigo, because the environment is so radically different. It operates by different rules and responds to different stimuli. Armed only with the perspectives and skills honed in traditional settings, one who tries to lead in a network environment can find the task unsettling and disorienting.[7]

The fear of organizational change can take on a life of its own. It becomes the fear of the unknown, fear of making a public mistake, fear of losing control, fear of having one's tried and true Rolodex taken away.

As one communications director said, "I know I need to change, I know that social media culture will lead to success, but I'm afraid and I just can't get unstuck from everything that I learned about controlling the message." The rules that she knew by heart are gone. The formulas that always worked, such as designating specific people to speak on behalf of her organization and courting mainstream media outlets to spread her message, no longer succeed. She can't bring herself to replace them with something as fluid and new as social media.

Another communications director joked that the biggest irony when it comes to social media is that "it's the only issue that legal and communications people agree on—that we can't do social media because we can't control it!"

Below is a list of the fears we have heard organizational leaders express that stop them from embracing social media. We wanted to list as many as possible in the hopes that by acknowledging them we will help people take the first step in overcoming them.

We fear social media because it will

- Make us look unprofessional if we show our human side and reveal unfinished plans and projects
- Compromise the quality of our work because of the likelihood of typos and poor grammar
- Open us up to public criticism we would rather pretend doesn't exist
- Hurt our organization's brand
- Open the floodgates of information that will overwhelm us
- Make senior staff more accessible to too many people who want their time
- Enable staffers or volunteers to write something that could be libelous
- Lead to someone lobbying on our behalf and compromise our tax-exempt status
- Encourage employees to spend enormous amounts of wasted time writing on Facebook, watching YouTube videos, and sending personal e-mails

Some of these fears are actually true. Blog posts will have typos in them, people will criticize an organization's efforts, and staffers will spend time watching YouTube videos. However, they aren't consequential and shouldn't stop organizations from embracing social media. Moreover, existing organizational policies such as confidentiality agreements, harassment policies, personnel policies, and Internet use policies already address some of these fears.

Organizations, particularly their leaders, need to talk about these issues forthrightly with staff. They need to look at how other organizations have opened themselves up and learned to live with and reduce these fears.

What they shouldn't do is then hand the social media toolkit over to the summer intern to "solve" the social media problem. Interns and young staffers can and should be engaged in helping to lead organizations into using social media, but not by themselves in a cubicle down the hallway. Organizational leaders need to learn for themselves why Twitter and Facebook may look identical from afar but feel very different when used. And the only way to do this is to get hands-on and use them. Organizational leaders must experience for themselves the pleasure, power, and excitement that come from connecting with friends and strangers online around a common issue or purpose.

PERSONAL SOCIAL MEDIA USE

The good news for people hesitant about social media is that they are probably already using some of the tools. Nearly everyone uses e-mail, surfs the Web, and has a mobile phone. The next step for organizations is to understand how to use them strategically for social change. The starting point is personal practice.

Ellen Miller had to make the transition herself into the social world. She's a nonprofit leader with a forty-year career as an advocate for more open and accountable government practices. In 2006, Ellen became the cofounder of the Sunlight Foundation, which uses the power of the Internet to make information about Congress and the federal government more meaningful and accessible to citizens. To succeed in this new role, Ellen had to change her thinking about the way that she had worked and the role of her organization. She described her shift this way: "It was the classic lightbulb going on. I realized that this new medium was a way to engage people at far less cost and more effectively. But it meant that I had to give up the control that I had used in running organizations in the past. I had to be willing to be open and recognize that the old ways of working [were] not as effective as I would have liked them to be . . . If outreach to my community was one of my key responsibilities, and the goal of my organization, then using social media myself had to be a priority."[8]

It is easier for adults to begin to practice anything new privately, in a safe place, in order to make mistakes in their own way and time. However, practicing alone can be difficult. It is hard to know where to begin, and easy to get stuck uploading vacation pictures or trying to set up a Twitter or Facebook account. Adults trying to master social media need friends to help them.

Many people can help ease the pathway into social media, and they are easy to find. They are the interns, the younger staff members, the teenagers at home. All can become social media reverse mentors. And in a business context, young staffers can enhance their own leadership skills by organizing monthly brown bag lunches to demonstrate social media tools for the entire staff.

As with mastering anything, just one sitting won't do. Leaders will need to make it a regular day and time on their calendar, and practice for a few weeks or months to feel comfortable using social media with some fluency.

Over time, leaders will discover which tools they particularly like and feel comfortable using through experimentation and practice. Twitter may feel more productive than Facebook. Watching videos on YouTube may be more energizing than uploading pictures to Flickr. There are no right or wrong preferences for social media; whatever tools or channels work for one person are fine.

A new user will soon learn the rules and norms of behavior that grease the wheels of the online world. Sharing information and content is expected and applauded. Thanking others and giving credit are a given. Self-serving pronouncements or pitches are discordant. Deanna Zandt, author of *Share This! How You Will Change the World with Social Networking*, describes the best practice for sharing information on social networks as 30 percent about the individual and their organization, and the remaining 70 percent about sharing, applauding, and linking to the work of others.

Once people begin to use social media privately, their use invariably seeps into their professional lives. Reading blogs about personal hobbies and passions leads to blog reading about issues and causes. Connecting with personal friends on Facebook will lead to professional friending. This is simply the result of the gravitational pull of social media where the lines between people and institutions are blurred. Once this happens, the possible ways that social media can begin to be used within their institutions will become clearer for organizational leaders. At that point, they are ready to turn their attention to how they want to use social media for their efforts strategically and intentionally.

THE INTERNAL CONVERSATION

Holly Hight, a field organizer for an advocacy group in California, was comfortable using Twitter and Facebook in her personal life. She naturally began to use them as part of her organizing work as well. She was soon admonished by senior staff for "going off policy message" on these social media channels. When Holly pushed back, the organization began a series of internal conversations about the use of social media. Holly writes: "We are taking a few steps in this direction, primarily by challenging our internal culture of message control and creating space for conversations across departments."[9]

Holly's situation points to specific questions all organizations have when considering a social strategy. Wrestling with these questions is essential to engaging effectively with social media. Organizations will need to revisit the same issues over time to ensure that they are fully embracing social media.

The questions are as follows:

• **What are the appropriate boundaries between public and private information?** Many young people have few boundaries between their public and private lives, exacerbated by the megaphone of social media. These blurred boundaries can be discomforting for older people brought up with norms of professional behavior that frowned upon revealing their personal lives publicly. However, social media is powered by conversations between real people. Ellen Miller faced this dilemma. She recalls, "I thought twice about taking down the veil between professional and personal, but then I plunged in and nothing terrible happened. Then I got used to it. The results of revealing a little bit about who you are and what you're interested in make you more attractive to other people."[10] Organizations automatically become more public because of social media. Holly Ross, the executive director of the Nonprofit Technology Network, explained why: "That's because social media does not just enable conversations. It enables *public* conversations."[11] No clear-cut rules for determining the lines between public and private information exist. Every organization and staffer has to develop a balance between public and private information individually. It is incumbent upon staffers to use their common sense when sharing and revealing information about themselves and their organizations online, and to remember that they are creating a permanent digital footprint wherever they go. Organizational leaders need to challenge their own fears and assumptions about what is appropriate to share online, while also remembering that authenticity is critical to online relationship building.

• **How do we balance our interest in being open with the technical needs to safeguard against cyber attacks?** We don't envy the information technology professionals whose jobs it is to keep organizations safe from hackers and spammers in a social world that requires openness. Matt Sharp, the information technology director of The David and Lucile Packard Foundation, describes the tension this way: "We have to get people across a river of scorpions without getting stung."[12]

Conversations between the information technology team and other departments around this issue should happen early and often. It is important that adversarial stances not be taken. All participants deserve opportunities to openly share what they need to be successful, and what the risks and rewards are of behaving in certain ways. The good news is that with technology there are always many ways to skin a cat. Organizations need to keep experimenting and looking for methods, tools, and approaches that balance safety and openness.

- **Will we be living in the Wild West if we open ourselves up online?** Using social media does not mean that organizations have to operate without any rules or expectations for civil behavior. Organizations are allowed to set the rules of engagement with their networks, particularly on their own blogs. After a particularly vicious personal attack on blogger Kathy Sierra in 2007, Tim O'Reilly posted a Blogger's Code of Conduct,[13] which offers seven suggestions to promote civil conversation online:

  1. Take responsibility not just for your own words, but for the comments you allow on your blog.
  2. Label your tolerance level for abusive comments.
  3. Consider eliminating anonymous comments.
  4. Ignore the trolls.
  5. Take the conversation offline and talk directly, or find an intermediary who can do so.
  6. If you know someone who is behaving badly, tell them so.
  7. Don't say anything online that you wouldn't say in person.

Organizations need to develop their own policies of online engagement and revisit them over time. However, when doing so, take care not to shy away from criticism.

- **How much do we have to be "on" with social media?** The always-on social media world doesn't actually have to be always on for people or organizations. It's important to engage with communities online somewhere, to invest in them and share with them; otherwise, they will never gain traction. That said, organizations don't have to live online 24/7 to be social. Socialness is judged from the outside by a willingness to be open and authentic, to connect and share. Regular engagement online is crucial, but one person doesn't have to be responsible for responding on Twitter at midnight every night. Share and spread out the work, and set reasonable, sustainable expectations for being "on."

- **Who should operate the channels?** Everyone should, and anyone could, and whoever wants to can. Social media use is not restricted to a particular department or position. The key, again, is authenticity. Real people need to do their own talking.

Logos don't tweet or blog or have real conversations with people. If the CEO is not actually sending messages using Twitter, then there shouldn't be a Twitter account with her name on it giving that impression. If the communications director or the intern is tweeting, then they should be identified as such in their profiles and not pretend to be someone else.

Julia Rocchi is the online communications manager for the United Nations Foundation. She tweets and blogs for the organization with the support of senior management. Her self-description on Twitter reads this way: "Big hair, big mouth, big plans. Writer, blogger, and Online Communications Officer at United Nations Foundation. Will hug/cook/travel at will." Julia is demonstrating straightaway that she is a real person who has likes and passions and even flaws (depending on what you think about big hair and a big mouth).

Previously, someone in Julia's position likely would have described herself as a "leading communications professional for the United Nations Foundation charged with engaging various audiences and interacting with the media community." With this description, we wouldn't have known Julia at all. She draws us in by revealing who she is and what makes her a fun, interesting person. Now, we can begin to connect with Julia and build a relationship with her based on our common interests as real people, not as organizational drones.

As the American Red Cross discovered, the answers to these questions become the basis for the formation of an organization's social media policy.

CODIFYING THE SOCIAL CULTURE

Once a social culture has taken root within an organization, it is important to encourage it by codifying it. Developing social media policies ensures that senior staff has fully embraced and taken responsibility for social media use. It also provides direction for individual staffers to know what they can and cannot do. These policies will change and evolve as social media tools develop over time.

"Laying down guidelines makes everyone think they have more control, and it help[s] everyone to feel better," says Wendy Harman of the American Red Cross. "In truth, our guidelines are quite vague. It goes on for a while but really just says, 'Use common sense and please don't say stupid stuff. In fact, we'd love it if you told your personal institutional story in a constructive way.'"[14]

Mashable is a Web site that provides social media guidance for organizations. They posted an outline of what should be included in social media guidelines:[15]

> A statement of purpose for the policies to encourage the use of social media.
> A reminder that everyone is responsible for what they write.

Encouragement to step out from behind the logo and be authentic.

A reminder of who the audiences are and what they mean to the organization.

An exhortation to use good judgment.

The need to balance personal and professional roles to help build community.

Respect for copyright and fair use.

The need to protect privacy, particularly of clients, and proprietary information.

The need to use social media in a way that adds value to the organization.

Creating a balance between online and on land activities.

Two of our favorite social media policies combine common sense with the real, human language of social media.[16] The first comes from a vice president of communications:

a. Don't write stupid stuff you'll regret some day, 'cause someday you'll regret it.

b. Don't moon people with cameras (or at least hide your face when you do).

c. Avoid "Friending" your boss and any of his/her teenage children, nieces, or nephews.

d. Do your damndest to ignore posts by people that report to you (especially if they're supposed to be working and all they are doing is twittering stupid, irritating stuff all day long).

e. Don't flirt too much with people other than your spouse.

Except for (e), the majority of these things are not policy issues, but management issues. If you've got someone that is twittering all day long instead of working, it's not a function of social media, it's a management issue.

The second comes from the Disgruntled Employees Blog in the form of a message on Twitter:

Be professional, kind, discreet, authentic. Represent us well. Remember that you can't control it once you hit "update."

CONCLUSION

Shifting the culture of an organization is not just about having new ideas or working with new tools; it means actually thinking about the work and organization fundamentally differently. Organizations need to practice being social and engaging with the outside world.

As the culture begins to shift, the issues that had been taking up a lot of time in staff meetings—how to protect the organization, how to stay on message, how to avoid criticism online—lose their potency. Organizations begin to spend more of their time talking to people inside and outside of the organization about the work, about the network, and about the possibilities of what they could all do working together. In this way the work spreads out, individual organizations feel less burdened, and they allow new ideas and energy in.

REFLECTION QUESTIONS

Personal questions for organizational leaders about their comfort with social media:

- Are you open to trying new communications approaches and tools?

- Do you value the knowledge and skills of younger people on staff who may be skilled social media users?

- Do you have someone within your organization or a peer who is comfortable with social media and can provide one-on-one coaching?

- Do you have peers on Facebook, Twitter, or other social networks whom you follow and observe?

Questions to ask about your organization and its culture:

- Does your organization embrace mistakes, take calculated risks, and reward learning and reflection?

- Can your organization tolerate a "try it and fix it as we go" approach that emphasizes failing fast?

- Are improvements to the way work gets done met with "We've always done it this way?" Or does change happen through robust discussions?

- Does your organization equate informality and individuality with a lack of caring or professionalism?

- Are staff entrusted to respond rapidly to situations rather than crawling through endless checkoff and approval processes?

- Do you have a flexible IT department that can allow employees to install social media tools for their work?

- Does your organization have a "culture of rapid response"?

- Do you evaluate current processes and update them as needed?

- Is there a process to vet online donor, member, or stakeholder feedback? Or does the program department not interact with communications? And why?

- Does your organization have processes that involve many departments? Does it take weeks to approve a press release or a Web page? How can these processes be refined to allow for live conversations about real issues?

- Does the legal department prevent communications from occurring? What's the barometer? Is the protection worth it in the new environment?

Questions to assist in creating a social media policy:

- How will we address negative comments?

- What is our policy about employees' personal use of social networks?

- What is our policy about employees using social network and social media for work-related activities?

- What topics are acceptable for staff to talk about online, and what is off-limits?

- What is our privacy policy?

- When should a staffer ask for help in deciding what to do online?

chapter FIVE

Listening, Engaging, and Building Relationships

In 2006, Cecile Richards became the president of the Planned Parenthood Federation of America (PPFA). Ninety-three Planned Parenthood affiliates manage 850 health centers nationwide. They provide family planning and reproductive health care services, education, and information to millions of people each year. Her charge was big and bold: to remake this sprawling system into a cohesive network of organizations.

Cecile's vision of remaking the organization meant opening up the organization's closed culture, the product of the confidentiality their services required and the constant cacophony of loud protests about its work. As she recalled, "Confidentiality is a big part of Planned Parenthood's culture. And, as you know, being successful with social media is the opposite of that. Three years ago, not everyone was convinced that we needed to shift our investment into our online presence. However, given that we're trying to reach young people, how could we ignore the place where most of them get their information?" Cecile's first challenge was to allay the board's fears that the dark underbelly of the Web would overwhelm their work. The organization also had to prove to women online that its efforts to listen and talk with them were sincere.

PPFA's Web site was the first place to begin building relationships. The Web site shared information about the organization, explained the issues for which it advocates, and perhaps most important, provided easy ways for people to find local health centers—information that had been difficult for people to access before. It was a first step in opening up the organization online, but it wasn't yet a conversation.

59

The next step for PPFA was to go to the places online where their audience naturally congregated, particularly Facebook and MySpace, and connect with them. But it didn't go smoothly at first. Tom Subak, the organization's vice president of online services, remembers, "We had to stop cramming calls to action down people's throats." The organization had to learn to work differently on social networking sites. Instead, Tom says, "we worked differently on social networking sites by creating a platform for folks to have a dialogue in the way they want. We support it and guide it."[1]

Today Facebook and MySpace host significant Planned Parenthood communities where individuals share their personal stories in their own words, images, and videos. The organization facilitates some of these conversations, but it also lets them go where people want them to go. The focus on these channels is to build relationships and trust. For instance, PPFA offers personal birthday wishes to its online Facebook friends as a way to let them know it cares about them as people, not just as potential ATM machines.

In partnership with the Kaiser Family Foundation and MTV, PPFA implemented an aggressive public information campaign in April 2009 to recognize National STD Awareness Month. The campaign focused on the need for sexually active young adults to be tested at Planned Parenthood health centers for sexually transmitted diseases. MTV aired public service announcements, and PPFA encouraged organizations and bloggers to post a widget on their sites that accessed an online chat desk—staffed by PPFA—to answer questions. The result: testing rates increased more than 50 percent during the month of April 2009 over April 2008. And in many places, such as North Carolina, Georgia, and St. Louis, Missouri, the number of men going to Planned Parenthood facilities for testing increased by 100 percent over the same period the previous year. PPFA viewed all those tested as possible new relationships for the organization online.

Backed by these successes, Planned Parenthood is making a remarkable journey into the social networking world. The organization trusted that most people have good intentions online and want to engage in conversations about their work. The people have proved them right. PPFA is now connecting with younger women and men whom they probably would not have reached on land. And as the organization develops these relationships over time, it is in the process of patiently moving people from talking to clicking to giving and advocating on their behalf.

Although PPFA is succeeding by building relationships using social media, the pressure to monitor and measure results has led many other nonprofit organizations to overemphasize transactions at the expense of relationship building. To fight this unintended consequence, organizations need to find a balance between raising money and forming connections.

Building a network of supporters who can do a variety of things for the organization at a moment's notice takes time and patience. Charlene Li, the founder of the Altimeter Group, summarizes the shift from transactional thinking to relationship building as moving from occasional, impersonal, short-term connections to passionate, constant, intimate, loyal ones.[2]

Online relationship building begins with listening and then moves to engagement and finally action. In this chapter, we will discuss this progression and also present a visual framework—a ladder of engagement—that can help organizations become intentional about their relationship-building efforts.

LISTENING

The key ingredient for building any relationship is good listening. Rather than just talking to, or worse, *at* people online, organizations first should listen to what people are talking about, what interests or concerns them, and how they view the organization. Listening is a terrific way for organizations to orient themselves online. It also helps organizations that are nervous or concerned about opening themselves up online to ease their way in.

However, listening is not simply scanning a river of unstructured data. The process involves sifting through online conversations on multiple channels like social networks and blogs. The value of listening comes from making sense of the data and using it to identify influencers, the key leverage points for spreading an organization's message and efforts far and wide. As Danielle Brigida, a social media strategist for National Wildlife Federation, says, "Paying attention to what people are saying is beneficial because it makes it easier for your organization to be relevant. Listening helps you be less of a spammer and more of a service provider."[3]

Social media makes listening to large numbers of people easy and inexpensive, unlike surveys and focus groups. Listening tools include **Google Alerts,** Technorati blog mentions, **RSS readers,** Twitter search, Delicious **tags,** and Boardreader (a Web site that shows posts on forums by keywords). Organizations can streamline listening by identifying the network hubs. These reliable reporters have already filtered and verified information within the network, making them trusted resources for information.

Yes, listening takes time, but don't think of it as time taken away from other activities. Rather, it's time invested in relationships, which are critically important to the organization's future well-being.

Lastly, listening is not the purview of a particular department or function within an organization. Pro Bono Net is a national nonprofit organization with nineteen staff people dedicated to providing online resources for legal aid and pro bono attorneys, law professors and students, and related social services advocates. Everyone in the organization engages in online listening. Project coordinator Kate Bladow described their efforts this way: "Overall, our goal for listening is to stay aware of what is happening in our niche, keep an eye out for opportunities, and learn more about what is happening with our partners."[4]

ENGAGING THE PUBLIC

The transition from listening to interacting with people online is the art of engagement. Engagement can be thought of as simply "being human through your computer," and organizations have a host of methods and techniques available to make that happen. They can share information, enter or initiate conversations, thank people for their efforts, educate and raise awareness of an issue, and of course, sometimes ask people to do something such as attend a rally or make a donation.[5]

Kate Bladow describes how Pro Bono Net moves from listening to engagement online: "[H]ow we act on the information depends on our personal style. Most of us act as aggregators, posting articles to news feeds that our community follows. As appropriate, we may comment on blog posts or pass links along to the right person to comment. . . . Another colleague is really good about using stories as an opportunity to reach out to partners and congratulate them or reconnect on a topic that she discussed with them previously."

An article posted online by *The Patriot Ledger* newspaper in Quincy, Massachusetts, on February 26, 2009, illustrates another powerful element of engagement: to clarify misperceptions about an organization.[6]

The article announced that the United Way of Massachusetts was giving two grants to community programs—one for $100,000 to the South Shore Day Care

Services, and another for $30,000 to Quincy Community Action Programs. Both grants were intended to help struggling families meet their heat, food, and other basic needs with free or low-cost services. The article was straightforward and dispassionate; the comments, however, were not.

The first commentator questioned why the United Way was making a donation to the day care center:

> Not understanding how this for-profit day care company gets to administer funds for food etc.? This is why I would never donate to United Way; the way they handle money astounds me. Too much temptation for directors etc. of companies who suddenly get this windfall of money from the good fairy. And who sets guidelines for the money? I always wonder if the people who donated their hard-earned dollars know how this money gets thrown around. Seems very odd to me.

The Day Care Center was listening and responded with a comment. They clarified the nonprofit organization's mission and programs, and described in more detail how funds are managed. The Day Care Center pointed to additional facts about their organization on the Web site. They ended with a promise to answer any additional questions.

Now engaged, the commentator had some follow-up questions:

> Yes this is a change from how South Shore Day Care operated in the past; I used your services some years ago when you were simply a day care provider. I had to pay going rate for day care which at that time was hundreds of dollars per week, despite the fact that I was a single parent beginning my career with a limited income.
>
> I am still curious how a day care provider is nonprofit. I will go to the website, thank you. I am happy to hear you are providing day care, and will be sure to recommend you to my daughters.

A representative from the United Way then provided additional clarification:

> Thanks for helping to clarify. I work at United Way. Another important point which might help, is that 100 percent of the funds we raise for the Community Support Fund are going back into the community for basic needs like rent, food, utilities etc. If you have any

other questions about the Community Support Fund, our accountability, or the guidelines we set for the quality agencies we support, feel free to call us directly. You can find our contact information at **http://supportunitedway.org**. This is money that is going to help local individuals and families who have been significantly impacted by the recession. If you know anyone who needs help, please advise them to call 2–1–1, our helpline.

We don't know if the commentator was ultimately swayed by the information provided. We do know that other readers of the article and the comments received more information than they would have had just from the news article. Perhaps someone felt differently about the United Way and the grantees as a result of the conversation.

Sometimes organizational leaders prefer to sit back and watch conversations unfold online about their issues and organizations. They view their role as a spectator sitting on the other side of a one-way mirror at a focus group. However, leaders should remember that their personal participation is crucial to relationship building. Conversations are personal interactions and opportunities to engage with people, correct misunderstandings, educate, and help spread the word. Everyone—including the listeners—needs to be engaged. And as the United Way example demonstrates, organizations have to be willing to do something online that they have often shied away from on land—namely, to engage with their critics.

CONVERSING WITH THE CRITICS

Criticism is always painful to hear, and online critics can be particularly vitriolic when hiding behind the anonymity of their screens. However, there are differences between a destructive attack, a demagogic appeal, and an honest disagreement with a critic of an organization. Refusing to engage in conversations, particularly critical ones, doesn't mean the criticism doesn't exist; it just means the organization is not willing to listen to it and engage with the critic.

Organizations must engage with critics who have legitimate concerns even when it feels uncomfortable. Criticism is an opportunity to learn and build relationships with the critics themselves. And social media are terrific vehicles for hearing criticism that may be too difficult for people to share in person or is often ignored in polite company.

The marketing expert Valeria Maltoni writes: "[P]eople ask me what happens if someone says you suck. I respond that I lean forward and ask them to tell me in how many ways I suck. Only when there's engagement is there sharing and communicating. When you refuse to take this step, you are the barrier."[7]

BUILDING STRONG RELATIONSHIPS

The purpose of listening and engaging is to build relationships between an organization and its supporters, potential supporters, and other organizations in their ecosystem. As Danielle Brigida at National Wildlife Federation says about building relationships as an organization, "I treat maintaining my professional relationships very similarly to how I maintain my personal friends. To me there is very little difference (everyone is my friend). I find time to incorporate them and I get to know what the person cares about and what their strengths are. I contact them when I have questions and I always am sure to follow up if I can."[8]

Building relationships online takes constancy and practice. Here are a few lessons we've discovered about relationship building online:

Losing control is more important than trying to gain it. One distinguishing characteristic of the digital world is that power is being pushed to the edges away from organizations and toward people. This shift is good for organizations that need to engage many people in their work; yet to successfully power the edges, organizations have to be willing to lose control.

"Losing control" is a frightening phrase; it connotes flying through space without a parachute or a net. In this respect, social media are kryptonite for people who feel a need to control their efforts too tightly. But the reality in our connected world is that spending energy trying to control what other people do and say is counterproductive.

Organizations still need to be intentional about their efforts, they still need messages and plans, but they also have to expect that people and organizations in their ecosystem will march to their own drummers. More important, imperfectly coordinated efforts can be enormously successful, even exhilarating, as they unfold in unexpected ways.

Only by letting go and throwing off the yoke of control can organizations unleash the power and creativity of many people to do amazing things on their behalf. Organizations need to follow the example of the Planned Parenthood

Federation of America and the American Cancer Society and many others who trusted their communities, lost control, and experienced great things.

Authenticity is crucial. As discussed previously, social media demands authenticity. The tools are the perfect vehicles for revealing one's true self and connecting in real, human ways across organizational boundaries. Conversely, a lack of authenticity can be devastating for organizational efforts online.

Having ulterior motives or pretending to be something or somebody you're not is not acceptable in these kinds of relationships. Such practices are called **astroturfing**, or fake attempts by organizations to build relationships. An astro-turfer may pay people to say nice things about someone or a company online without disclosing that they are paid agents. Organizations with shallower pockets may astroturf by having staff people pretend to be constituents or supporters.

Or maybe someone's ego is so big, their fear of criticism is so great, that he astroturfs for himself. Whole Foods founder and CEO John Mackey spent seven years astroturfing behind the pseudonym Rahodeb. Using this pseudonym, he posed as an investor on the Yahoo! Finance **message board,** acted as a cheerleader for Whole Foods, and demonized the competition.

Karma banking. Stand-alone organizations work hard to pull resources, information, and credit into their orbits. This does not work in a world powered by social media that draws news, activities, and conversations away from the organization and into the ecosystem. Rather, it's best to send good things into the world without expecting an immediate return, thus building the social capital integral to long-term social change. This process is called "karma banking," a phrase coined by Tom Watson, author of *CauseWired*.[9] Of course, organizations are allowed to take credit when appropriate. There is nothing inherently wrong with being self-interested. The problems begin when self-interest is exercised at the expense of others.

Networked Nonprofits are energetic karma bankers. They use a variety of social media to share information with their network, celebrate others' achievements, and thank people often and loudly for their efforts. The highest compliment that a good karma banker can receive is "You're a great sharer."

Karma banking has a boomerang effect. When an organization needs something in the future like comments on a critic's blog, information forwarded about a new fundraising activity, or an introduction to a funder, there sits the karma bank, fat and overflowing, waiting to be used. Karma banks are storehouses of trust and reciprocity that organizations can draw on in the future.

People are good and helpful. Building strong relationships with supporters is built on the premise that people are good, trustworthy, and sincere in their desire to help. This axiom turned eBay into a global trading platform without the company having to scrutinize every transaction.

Some organizations pretend they don't have problems. Others believe that admitting their problems makes them seem weak to outsiders. Neither case is true. All organizations have problems, concerns, challenges, and difficulties. And all organizations can use outside help to think through issues, develop creative solutions, and connect to other networks and resources.

However, organizations also need humility to not presume that they know all the answers and to be able to ask their networks for help. Networked nonprofits that have built strong relationships with large numbers of people have found that they can draw on these relationships for energy and creativity to help them to thrive.

There is no one-size-fits-all friendship. Social media tools cannot create friendships. Only people do that through their communications and connections. That said, social media can enhance and augment different degrees of friendship. Of course, long-term friendships have a different level of intensity and emotional resonance than a friend made on Facebook last week. But that doesn't mean the new friend on Facebook isn't a valuable new addition to a life, a cause, and an organization.

We never know the pathways that friendships are going to take, so we shouldn't try to predict or pigeonhole them. In the same way, social networks have their own rhythms that organizations can only follow and support, not create or dictate. Stephanie McAuliffe of The David and Lucile Packard Foundation observed, "Network effectiveness is about ebb and flow of tides. It's important to build your network before you need it. And sometimes networks will hum along at a lower level of activity. . . . While the network is just 'networking' or is engaging in basic activities, it is building the trust needed for the network to activate, moving into action mode to solve something when the window of opportunity arises."[10]

It is impossible to know what resources, knowledge, or personal connections an individual or organization can bring to your organization without getting to know them better. But such unpredictability doesn't mean that organizations shouldn't aim to strategically increase supporter engagement. And they can achieve this through a model that we call a **ladder of engagement**.

THE LADDER OF ENGAGEMENT

Organizations have a rich mix of supporters, from the lightly touched to the superenergized. They need to create bite-size steps to engage supporters in their cause and help them become more active doers, cheerleaders, and donors if they so choose. Using a framework that we call a ladder of engagement can help organizations better understand and assess their efforts of moving more people to deeper levels of involvement (see Figure 5.1).

The levels of engagement are defined as follows:

- **Happy bystanders,** including blog readers, friends on Facebook, and personal acquaintances such as coworkers.

- **Spreaders,** people who are willing to share information about a cause with other people.

- **Donors,** who contribute financially to a cause.

- **Evangelists,** who reach out to their personal social networks and ask other people to give time and money to the cause.

- **Instigators,** who create their own content, activities, and events on behalf of the cause. Instigators may even create a new cause or organization to more fully express themselves.

As previously discussed in Chapter Three, "Understanding Social Networks," a very small group of people will always do the overwhelming amount of work for any effort, and a very large group of people will do little bits. This means any effort will have far more happy bystanders than evangelists. The ladder provides a framework for envisioning the types of participation that organizations need to be successful. But the growth doesn't just happen. Organizations must be intentional about building strong relationships with their supporters and helping them step up the ladder of engagement.

Every person is capable of deepening her engagement with a cause that has sparked her interest at a particular time. However, it is critically important that organizations not judge participants by their involvement at a time

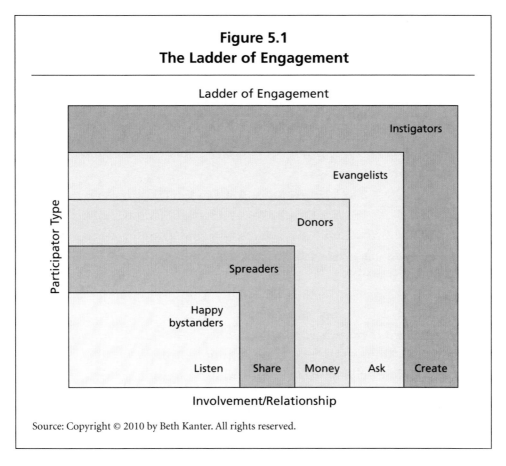

Figure 5.1
The Ladder of Engagement

Ladder of Engagement

Participator Type

Instigators

Evangelists

Donors

Spreaders

Happy
bystanders

Listen | Share | Money | Ask | Create

Involvement/Relationship

in which it may be difficult for them to engage fully. Someone could care about the cause deeply but not have time at a particular moment to help out. At another time, though, an e-mail from a friend crosses his screen, the stars of passion and time align, and the person gets so moved that he organizes a house party to inform his friends about the cause—and organizes a separate silent auction as well.

Priscilla Brice-Weller, a blogger and activist from Australia, reflected on building relationships this way: "I think that the best way to encourage supporters to become activists is simply to ask them how they want to be more involved. Sometimes when I do this, they are honored that I've asked. Other times, they apologize that they can't help right now because of personal circumstances. Nobody has abused me yet, so I'll remain with this strategy for now and will let you know in time how I get on!"[11]

The ladder is not a linear progression from one step on the ladder to another. People can start anywhere and work their way up or down. They can take one step at a time or hopscotch their way around the ladder. Again, organizations can't control what people do; they can only provide ample opportunities for people to enjoy where they are on the ladder and become more engaged if they so choose.

CONCLUSION

Organizations don't have any resources to squander. The problems are too difficult and the needs too great to turn away anyone interested in helping. Even if organizations had unlimited resources, working alone cuts them off from the creativity and ingenuity of the many people in the ecosystem affected by or interested in their work.

Moreover, in order to build strong relationships, organizations must open themselves to network input and assistance and allow it to alter and improve their plans. Organizations have to treasure their relationships with people and value what they bring to the effort. Organizations need to be patient, resilient, and resourceful in building relationships with many people in many different ways. And they need to appreciate these efforts honestly, sincerely, and publicly.

REFLECTION QUESTIONS

Listening

- What are people saying about your organization, brand, programs, or issues in social media spaces?
- What keywords should you be using to search for or connect with people in social spaces?
- What is the tone, volume, and sentiment of the feedback?
- What is true? What can you improve?
- What is a perception that needs correction?
- Have you identified the influencers in your community?

Engaging

• Based on your listening, what types of conversations do you need to have with your audience?

• Are you asking questions?

• Are you responding in a way that is helpful? Kind? Polite?

• Are you sharing useful information (not just pointing to your own content)?

• Are you asking for feedback in the early stages?

Relationship Building

• What are your touch points with audiences? Are you communicating only to ask for money, and even then in an impersonal way?

• Do you reward or recognize influencers on social media spaces who care about your issues?

• Are you saying thank-you for little things in a nice way, and meaning it?

Building Trust Through Transparency

Organizations have developed tools for monitoring their progress. One of these tools is the dashboard, a series of measures that managers can compare month to month, such as the number of visitors or the number of beds occupied. Dashboards are concise, and often provide visual and compelling ways to get a snapshot of organizational performance at any point in time. And they are almost always kept private for internal use by staff and boards.

But what if these reports were shared more broadly? What if the default setting was for nonprofit organizations to share dashboard reports or results metrics with everyone? The Indianapolis Art Museum took that plunge in 2007 when it posted its institutional dashboard on its Web site for everyone to see.[1]

The impetus for opening up the museum's institutional performance to the public came from Maxwell Anderson, the museum's chief executive officer. Before his arrival in 2006, the Indianapolis Museum of Art had been a traditional museum, open to the public for viewing the artwork, but closed to the public in terms of its management. Anderson felt strongly that the institution had to become more open for the public to better understand how it operated, what difficulties the organization faced, and what steps it was taking to improve its performance.

According to Rob Stein, the museum's chief information officer, "Max felt that if we were closed, we'd hide behind rationalizations for why certain things were broken. I think all organizations have these broken areas. It's been refreshing to work in a culture where honesty and transparency about them is encouraged as a step toward continuous improvement."[2]

73

Naturally the staff and board had concerns about making the dashboard public. But the new leadership was steady and encouraging in its support of the effort. Stein says, "The dashboard is both a way to communicate to donors and the press the truth behind how we're running the museum, but also a crucial tool for staff members to track their own performance over time, knowing that the world is potentially watching."

The dashboard (Figure 6.1) tracks the museum's progress against a series of key indicators such as the number of visitors, monthly membership rates, energy efficiency, visitors' geographic location, and how many works of art are on loan or exhibit. Online viewers can click on any of the data points and read more about the museum's strategy relating to that area.

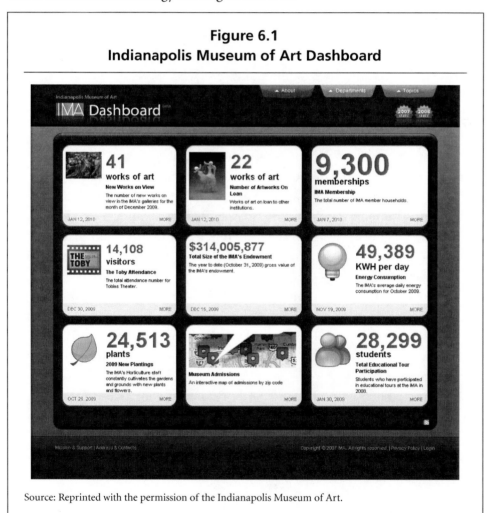

Figure 6.1
Indianapolis Museum of Art Dashboard

Source: Reprinted with the permission of the Indianapolis Museum of Art.

At first glance, the attractive display of data points might seem transactional rather than insightful. What does it really mean after all that 13,833 people visited the Tobias Theater in the first half of 2009? But the museum transforms itself into a different kind of organization when one clicks on the data point. That click shows anybody—a funder, volunteer, artist, or visitor—the trends over time. By revealing themselves in this level of detail, the organization invites the public to work with them to think about and try to understand what is working, what isn't, and why.

For instance, the museum is particularly concerned about energy consumption. The need to balance its goal to conserve energy with the stringent temperature and humidity requirements for preserving the artwork is difficult. It requires constant monitoring to assess whether the balance is being met. The dashboard tracks this data point as the daily consumption of energy by the museum. Tracking these data over time, we learn that the staff reduced the average monthly electricity and natural gas usage over 30 percent since the beginning of 2006.

But what happens when the numbers, particularly for fundraising or endowment size, don't go in the right direction? Stein notes, "We've certainly had our share of bad data to share in the last twelve months. The total value of our endowment took a significant beating as demonstrated in the online statistic. Couple that fact with our contributed support numbers which are displayed there, and it's clear that this has not been the best financial period for the IMA.

We also went through a restructuring, which resulted in the elimination of a number of staff positions, which is also indicated online. There were some gut-churning moments putting those numbers up, but they are really the proof of the pudding and demonstrate that the dashboard isn't just a spin exercise for the museum's PR department. On a positive note, sharing the negative statistics accurately gives us a *great* platform to talk to donors and funding agencies about the realities of the IMA's financial situation. It's great to let the facts make the case for you."[3]

The museum uses its blog to discuss the dashboard findings and to discuss the museum's status, upcoming activities, and what they are learning over time. Museum staff also talks on Twitter with the public.

Reflecting on his organization's embrace of transparency, Stein had this to say: "The 'openness' is a hair shirt that encourages us to stay on the straight-and-narrow, an external motivation to continue to do the right thing even when it has a negative appearance on the surface."

For nonprofit organizations to work successfully as a network with others in their ecosystem, they have to be open and transparent. Transparency is not a buzzword or a system; it is a way of thinking and being for organizations. They must be brutally honest with themselves about whether and how they are open internally and externally. They need to challenge themselves to do a better job of sharing information about results beyond their boardroom. And they should not only solicit, but also honor public input by using and responding to it.

In this chapter, we will define and explore the three categories of nonprofit transparency. We will also identify ways that organizations can practice transparency using social media.

WHY TRANSPARENCY AND WHY NOW?

Greater transparency is vital for nonprofit organizations that want to embrace a broader network of individuals and organizations. Engaging more honestly and openly with the networked world cannot happen without significant organizational transparency.

The nonprofit sector has been slow to adopt almost any level of transparency. A study on voluntary disclosure practices by nonprofits conducted by Guidestar, an online repository of information on hundreds of thousands of nonprofits, revealed that only 43 percent of the nonprofits surveyed posted their annual reports on their Web sites. Thirteen percent posted their audited financial statements, and a minuscule 3 percent posted their respective IRS letters of determination on their Web sites.[4]

It is tempting to grade organizations as either transparent or not. However, transparency is more complicated than a simple grade can convey. It is not a zero-sum game for organizations. Certainly organizations should hit at least the threshold of engagement, but beyond that is a sliding scale of openness that changes with the circumstances and needs of an organization and its network.

For example, organizations should be easily understood from the outside and easy to navigate once inside. But this does *not* mean that every conversation, piece of paper, and decision requires public scrutiny. As technology pioneer Esther Dyson said, "You cannot be fully transparent all the time because you need to give people a safe place to have the discussion without disrespecting others."[5]

Chris Anderson, editor-in-chief of *Wired* magazine and author of *The Long Tail* (2006) and *Free* (2009), confirmed this notion: "Radical transparency is the ultimate aim, but each company is going to have to find their own path to that themselves that reflects their corporate culture, their own competitive risk, and more important, who their participants are or could be. My point is: try being more transparent rather than less, and see what happens."[6]

In order to begin a conversation about transparency, each organization must determine its own starting point.

THREE KINDS OF ORGANIZATIONS

Nonprofit organizations fall into three broad categories of transparency. The first is the **Fortress**.

Fortress organizations sit behind high walls and drawn shades, holding the outside world at bay to keep secrets in and invaders out. Self-protection is normative behavior inside of Fortresses: "This is the way we do things here, this is how we dress, and how we communicate with one another." Where there's an "us," there must be a "them."

Fortress organizations keep "them" outside the gates by using their versions of moats and drawbridges. Everything, particularly communication, goes from the Fortress outward, but nothing comes back in. Devices designed to keep people out include plans developed only by staff, press releases, closed meetings, and unexplained decision making. Forms, approvals, committees, and sign-offs are bureaucratic speed bumps that keep Fortresses moving at glacial speed.

Fortress organizations have risk-averse DNA, the resulting physics of putting people together in one space who are primarily concerned about their own reputations and continued employment. Caution becomes the prevailing operating philosophy in most of these organizations. Fortresses assume the worst about people; it is what their leaders consider the most prudent way of working. Better safe than sorry, they believe, and safe means keeping your distance.

Fortresses are the stereotypical institutions, government agencies or monopolies, that we interact with because we have little or no choice. Fortresses, however, are not the sole purview of the for-profit and government sectors; a significant number of nonprofit organizations can also be classified as Fortresses.

The second category of organizations is **Transactionals**. Transactional organizations provide services offered and selected by the public primarily based on cost. For instance, airline travelers may prefer to fly on JetBlue or Southwest

Airlines, but they will choose another airline—dirty seats, unpleasant staff, and all—because the ticket price is lower for that particular flight.

Transactional nonprofit organizations see people on the outside as serving one purpose: to write checks.

They constantly check the turnstiles for the number of people who attended an event or donated, the number of volunteers who showed up, or the number of beds that were filled. In the transactional mind-set, checking off these isolated interactions is the same as fulfilling the organization's mission. Although they are changing, United Ways and the United Jewish Appeal were known to have transactional relationships with their communities.

Being a transactional organization doesn't mean that is the only way that they work. It means that the predominant mode of operating focuses on transactional interactions with people outside of the organization's walls.

The third category is **Transparents**.

The opposite of Fortresses, Transparents could be considered glass houses, with the organizations presumably sitting behind glass walls. However, this isn't real transparency because a wall still exists. True transparency happens when the walls are taken down, when the distinction between inside and outside becomes blurred, and when people from the outside are let in and staffers are let out.

Transparency is even stronger when the high walls and closed doors are not created in the first place. We can think of transparency like a sponge in the ocean. The scientific name for sponges is Porifera, which means "pore bearing." These simple organisms let up to twenty thousand times their volume in water pass through them every day as they breathe and eat.[7] But because they are also anchored to the ocean floor, the sponges can withstand the open, constant flow without inhibiting it.

Transparent organizations behave like these sponges. They are anchored, they are clear about what they do, and they know what they are trying to accomplish. However, they still let people in and out easily, and are enriched in the process. This can only happen when organizations trust that people on the outside have good intentions, a key ingredient for relationship building.

Organizations are transparent when

- Leadership is straightforward when talking to various audiences.

- Employees are available to reinforce the public view of the organization and to help people when appropriate.

- Their values are easily seen and understood.

- Their culture and operations are apparent to everyone inside and out.

- They communicate all results, good and bad.

Transparent organizations consider everyone inside and outside of the organization resources for helping them to achieve their goals. Jake Brewer, the engagement director for the Sunlight Foundation, describes his organization's efforts to be transparent this way: "We often ask in team meetings, 'How can the community help with this?' or 'How can this be more open?' The result is that instead of an internal e-mail that only the team sees, all of our Twitter followers see it along with our staff."[8]

THE SMITHSONIAN INSTITUTION PRACTICING TRANSPARENCY

Night at the Museum: Battle of the Smithsonian opened in the spring of 2009 in movie theaters across the country. In the film, the Smithsonian Institution comes to life in great and joyful ways. Amelia Earhart flies her plane daringly across The Mall, while the national monuments come to life and wander around the city. This peek inside the museum mirrored the organization's efforts to open up its strategic planning process on the Web for the public to see and join in.

Transparency can become part of the processes for ensuring that staff and the public have opportunities to help shape prospective efforts. The Smithsonian Institution's open strategic-planning process for its digital media program is just such an example.

All previous planning efforts had taken place behind closed doors. But that was before the crisis. In 2008, the Smithsonian ousted then-president Lawrence M. Small for financial mismanagement. When the new president, G. Wayne Clough, was announced, he said, "I know the Smithsonian, for many people in their minds, is about the past. But it is not. It is about America's future."[9]

Clough was adamant about making new media a strategic focal point in the Smithsonian's future. And Michael Edson, the Smithsonian's chief information officer of web and new media, became the moving force behind shaping the Institution's open planning process.

The Smithsonian began with a series of facilitated discussions at face-to-face workshops. The workshops included Smithsonian staff as well as representatives from all the different constituencies it was trying to reach. Each workshop also included real-time transcriptions of the proceedings posted on the Web site.

Information generated from the workshops was then shared on a wiki where the public could evaluate, sift, weigh, and consider the ideas. Smithsonian leaders wrote an open letter and posted it on the wiki to explain what they were doing and why:

> We think most planning strategies fail because of five classic mistakes, which, with your help, we intend to avoid:
>
> - Strategic planning is conceived as a static, once-every-five-years activity.
> - The strategy is too ambitious for the skills and capacity of the organization.
> - Nobody translates the strategy into actionable tactics.
> - There is insufficient data/metrics/analysis to guide decisions upstream or evaluate tactical success downstream.
> - Ownership of the strategy is ambiguous and intermittent.

The letter continued,

> This is an experiment, not without risk. Inevitable gaffes, missteps, and boneheaded mistakes will be confined to the neutral zone of the wikispaces domain, not enshrined under the www.si.edu banner.[10]

The Smithsonian continued its outreach and data gathering by asking the following question on YouTube:

> Given the new ways of acquiring and sharing knowledge through technology—the Internet, social networking, video sharing, and cell phones—where do you see the Smithsonian's museums and websites going in the future? How can we make education more relevant to you in a digital age?

Ninety people uploaded videos to YouTube with their aspirational wishes for the Smithsonian.

As Smithsonian staffer Marc Bretzfelder commented on Beth's Blog, "getting an institution as large as ours to undertake an integrated approach to New and Social Media requires building our systems from the ground up to both meet the internal needs of our researchers and other specialists. We need to begin to get a view from a lot of perspectives, and this is just one more slice of the pie."[11]

Making a shift to working in more open and porous ways is not easy. But steps can be taken at the outset that can help ease the transition.

WORKING IN TRANSPARENT WAYS

In full-throated Reaganesque form, our message to Fortresses and Transactionals is, "Take down those walls!" Of course, it's one thing to rise from your chair and declare it, and quite another to actually do it.

What follows are examples of ways that organizations can become more transparent, accessible, and understandable to people on the outside. At the most fundamental level in this connected world, organizations need to be find-able. The author and blogger Jeff Jarvis explains, "Living in public today is a matter of enlightened self-interest. You have to be public to be found. Every time you decide not to make something public, you create the risk of a customer not finding you or not trusting you because you're keeping a secret. Publicness is also an ethic. The more public you are, the easier you can be found, the more opportunities you have."[12] Specifically, Jarvis is referring to organizations ensur-ing that their Web sites are easily found by **search engines** such as Google. Publicness also happens when organizations create blogs that allow comments and have a presence on social networking sites such as Facebook that make them easy to find by strangers.

Another place to start becoming more transparent is by letting go of an organi-zation's information. The old economy assumed value in keeping materials locked away. Organizations looked for ways to create revenue streams by requiring people to pay for content such as curricula or training materials. In reality, this approach raised very little money yet reinforced Fortress-like defenses.

Organizations don't have to wait for people to ask for their information; they can post it online themselves. The law requires board minutes be available upon request. They can be posted online rather than waiting for people to ask for them.

Organizations that are not making basic regulatory reports available are play-ing a desultory game of push me, pull you. For instance, as with board minutes, the IRS determination letter must be made available upon request. So why not just push it out rather than make someone pull it out of the organization?

Organizations can also go beyond their tax reports and reveal exactly how much money they received from individual, corporate, and foundation donors. If someone asks for his or her contribution to remain anonymous, that's fine; but most people are proud of their donations and would happily see them acknowledged.

And while we're posting things, why not post financial audits *with* the management letters, plus strategic plans, evaluation plans, reports, and any other plans that you have?

Universities are posting curricula online and offering video lectures for free. Open source software applications such as Firefox have their code open to programmers to make it better.

Organizations can let their content go without losing control of it entirely. Creative Commons is a growing licensing movement that frees up content from restrictive copyright laws. It enables creators to share their content however they choose, giving their materials and tools a wider audience in a respectful, fair way. For instance, an organization may post its training curriculum for others to use, but ask for attribution when they do so. Or it may require a fee for its use, or simply let the content go and ask that users share any improvements they make.

The Environmental Defense Fund has energetically let go of its content. The organization uses Creative Commons licenses on its Web site to encourage others to use its materials with attribution. It shares training materials on its site and through a Web site for sharing presentations called Slideshare. It posts strategy documents on the blog and shares them as Google documents. Staffers at the Environment Defense Fund also share their research with their network and ask for help in developing it further. Dave Witzel, the director of the organization's Innovation Exchange, says that this is the best way for the organization to blur the lines between their internal and external work.

Indeed, transparency is not just an external exercise with the public; it is also important for organizations to open up and share information internally with staff. One thorny issue for many organizations is whether to share information about salaries. Contrary to conventional wisdom, salaries are not always locked away and hidden from view. We know what movie stars and ballplayers are paid. We know what executives at public companies earn. Union and government salaries are also public information. A few years ago, the salaries of top executives at nonprofits began to be reported on the IRS tax forms.

None of these organizations or institutions has crumbled as a result of salary transparency. Organizations that resist sharing this information do so because of an outdated, Victorian sense of politeness or a fear they will open up a Pandora's box of unrest and distraction. Unrest and distraction don't come from revealing information; they come from keeping it secret.

More information about salaries is already on the Web through the 990 tax forms or Web sites such as Glassdoor.com, where people can anonymously submit salary information for particular companies. Ed Lawler, director of the Center for Effective Organizations at the Marshall School of Business at the University of Southern California, said employees will feel cheated and undervalued in the absence of reliable information on how they are paid in comparison to others within the organization.[13]

If organizations want staff to feel fairly treated, they must deliver clarity, intentionality, and transparency in salaries. They must ensure that the reasons and thresholds for promotions and salary increases are clearly and openly explained.

Once started down this pathway, organizations will find myriad ways of sharing information internally that reduce uncertainty and increase trust within the organization. As a result, they can loosen the tight ties—the clusters of people who know things versus those left out in the cold—that turn organizations into Fortresses.

CREATING A TRANSPARENT FUTURE

The future of an organization has to be as transparent as the past. A good way to start is with internal conversations about how the organization works. Who makes strategic decisions within the organization, and can they be appealed if someone disagrees with them? How will we learn how well we are doing? How can we get more input from a wider variety of people? Organizations can begin these conversations internally and then share them externally with the organization's network of supporters, much like the Smithsonian Institution did.

Transparency also aids in organizational accountability. A blog by a senior executive can be enormously helpful in facilitating conversations about planning and in ensuring that those giving input feel heard, as part of ongoing, iterative conversations about how the organization operates. Let's imagine an organization has been accused of misusing public funds. In keeping with the old adage that the best defense is a good offense, the blog that the senior executive has been writing for the last year to share information about the organization now becomes a vehicle for addressing the criticism directly. The blogger can discuss the accusations and share the accounting process and continue an open dialogue with the public about the organization's finances.

In addition, by making their work public, organizations are pledging to do certain things in certain ways. The public can also join in group efforts like the ones we will discuss in Chapter Eight, "Working with Crowds." In this way, the public can hold the organization accountable, and the organization can hold their participants accountable for what they do and how they do it.

CONCLUSION

Organizations unaccustomed to letting information, documents, and processes go may find the transition to transparency discomforting. But the benefits of inviting people in and sharing in an organization's development far outweigh the potential downside. Imagine how much stronger the network's reactions, input, and suggestions will make your organization—and how exciting it will feel to share your great work with more people.

REFLECTION QUESTIONS

Information

- What financial information should you post and when?

- When could full disclosure hurt or help your organization?

- Does your organization know the line between being "open" and revealing trade secrets?

- Are there internal processes or conversations that would be appropriate to share for feedback at an earlier stage than you are sharing now?

- Are there opportunities to report on processes as they unfold to facilitate more feedback from stakeholders and improve the program?

Relationships

- Is your openness respectful and sensitive to other organizations or people?

- Are there any potential conflicts that could be fodder for public criticism?

- What is your strategy for addressing potentially difficult relationships?
- Are there relationships (or information about the relationships) that if made public could be damaging or embarrassing for your organization?

Employees

- Do you have clear and well-communicated policies so that employees know what the limits are—particularly around confidential information?
- What tools does management have in place to communicate with employees? Do they build trust?
- How can employees respond to this communication?
- Do your staff genuinely feel that their opinions and concerns matter and that their interests are heard? Are your staff champions for your organization away from the workplace?

Sharing Results

- How does your organization respond to inquiries?
- How does your organization test new methods and then share their results?
- Measure the number of times the organization's leaders are available to answer questions.

Making Nonprofit Organizations Simpler

"How it is possible that the richest country on earth has 20 percent of its children living in poverty?" Joan Blades and her friend Kristen Rowe-Finkbeiner asked. Their curiosity piqued, they began to dig deeper. They learned that the United States did not rank well in comparison to other industrialized countries in regard to infant mortality, paid family leave, paid sick leave, and quality, affordable child care and health care. For example, nearly 80 percent of low-wage workers do not have paid sick leave. For working mothers, this means they cannot afford to take care of their sick children. As Joan says, "A society that marginalizes its mothers impoverishes its children."[1]

Joan is the cofounder of MoveOn.org, and Kristen is a journalist and expert in the field of environmental policy and political strategy. They surveyed the landscape of organizations and people who work on public policy issues affecting mothers and their children. They saw advocacy groups, elected officials, and academics. They also saw one glaring, critical omission: mothers.

In 2006, they decided to put their grassroots organizing experience and social media savvy together and created a nonprofit organization called MomsRising.org.

Joan and Kristen began by listening to moms across the country. They attended coffees and parlor meetings—intentionally reaching out across the usual boundaries of income, education, geography, and religion—to hear them talk about their lives and struggles raising children with so many institutional barriers and policies in their way.

They broadened these conversations online using their blog to engage more people. They asked people to sign up on their Web site as members by asking for

Figure 7.1
MomsRising.org "Mother of the Year" Customizable Video

their e-mail addresses and ZIP codes. The membership wasn't fee-based, and all members received e-mail updates and action alerts.

After two years, MomsRising.org had about 160,000 members. In 2009, the organization created a video called "Mother of the Year" that people could send to mothers they knew (see Figure 7.1). The video went viral and was viewed over twelve million times. The resulting additional one million new members represented amazing growth for the organization in a very short time.

As remarkable as what MomsRising.org had done is what it had not done. The organization intentionally did not grow to become a large, bureaucratic organization. MomsRising.org has remained an intentionally simple organization by

- Having their staff of ten people all work virtually.

- Using social media tools whenever possible to simplify their work internally and engage in conversations with people in their network.

- Feeling comfortable following as well as leading. For instance, they listened to their members' wishes to add to their list of policy priorities stricter enforcement of federal standards ensuring that toys such as lead-laced Thomas the Tank Engines imported from China didn't make it into the country.

- Sticking to what they do best. Other organizations would have considered adding an advocacy department or arm to their organization. After all, without policy changes MomsRising.org ultimately will not be successful. But Kristen and Joan knew it was important for them to stick to what they do best—outreach to and organizing of moms. They have formed partnerships with dozens of advocacy groups to extend their network without pulling themselves off task. Joan said, "Our expertise is in working with our members and powering the grassroots. We have wonderful policy partners that are steeped in these issues. It's a win-win."[2]

A common refrain within nonprofit organizations and by nonprofit staffers is, "How can I make my life simpler when I have so much to do?" The answer is, well, simple: *You have too much to do because you do too much.*

Organizations and people do too much when they work within systems that are too complicated. Complexity slows organizations down and creates Byzantine structures that keep good ideas and energy outside their walls. However, making something complicated turns out to be pretty easy, while making something simple—whittling it down to its essence—is really hard. Even writing about simplicity is hard!

Simplicity clarifies organizations and forces them to focus their energy on what they do best, while leveraging the resources of their ecosystem for the rest. Simplicity powers more informal connections between people, blurs boundaries, and enables insiders to get out and outsiders to get in. Finally, simplicity helps to scale efforts because together, people can strengthen and improve communities better than a single organization ever could.

We will discuss in this chapter why organizations must move from complexity to simplicity to become Networked Nonprofits. We will also provide specific suggestions for ways that organizations and staffers can simplify their work.

WHY COMPLEXITY IS A BARRIER TO BECOMING A NETWORKED NONPROFIT

Our love affair with organizational complexity began long ago. Yochai Benkler wrote about organizations and their attraction to complexity this way: "The solution to this increased complexity in the late 19th, early 20th century was to increase the role of structure and improve its design. During the first two-thirds of the twentieth century, this type of rationalization took the form of ever-more complex managed systems, with crisp specification of roles, lines of authority, communication and control."[3]

As discussed in the second chapter, nonprofit organizations were not immune from the trend toward organizational complexity. As the twentieth century wore on, they became more bureaucratic and hierarchical, more like fortresses and less like transparent organizations. Not all professionalization was bad for nonprofit organizations. Improved financial accounting, for example, benefits both the organizations and the people who regulate and fund them. But too many organizations took to heart the presumption that adding more layers, decision points, moats, and gateways was the best way to try to fulfill their missions.

Margaret Wheatley summarizes the process of organizations becoming more complex: "Things that were simple, like neighborly conversations, have become a technique, like intergenerational, cross-cultural dialogue. Once a simple process becomes a technique, it can only grow more complex and difficult."[4] The growth of individual organizations made them bigger, more expensive, and harder to manage and sustain. It didn't, by definition, make them more effective.

The international consulting firm Booz Allen Hamilton conducted a study on the downsides of organizational complexity for nonprofit organizations. The paper, entitled "Victims of Success: Reducing Complexity for Nonprofits," stated that as nonprofit organizations became larger, their leadership didn't understand how the work was done. Field-level managers didn't understand how their roles fit into the larger organizational picture. And organizations often changed their mission or strategy at the behest of donors.[5]

Complexity stems in part from the desire to control internal and external environments as much as possible. Complexity creates the distractions that make organizational life crazy making in its inefficiency. It's all the time spent discussing who is responsible for doing what rather than just doing it. It is all the energy spent trying to control messages, people, and brands. Take a moment to imagine how different organizational life could be if we stopped spending time discussing who can and can't go to particular meetings, and just made them open to everyone.

Complexity and the desire to control one's environment cause organizations to close themselves off from their ecosystem. This, in turn, creates a mad internal scramble for resources. According to the nonprofit blogger Michele Martin, nonprofits "are constantly talking about what we lack—money, information, staff, resources. There's a strong feeling that there isn't enough to go around, and so the focus is on grabbing the largest share possible for your organization and holding onto that share for dear life." Organizations trapped in this scarcity bubble define everyone else, out there, as competitors for resources.[6]

The opposite of scarcity is abundance. Organizations that connect with their ecosystems find their worlds filled with a variety of new resources. The ecosystem has within it people with expertise and creativity, willing volunteers, collaborative organizations, and potential donors. Organizations that focus on abundance rather than scarcity are also able to open themselves up to innovative approaches from their ecosystem. When unlocked from their competitive stances, organizations have opportunities to engage differently with people outside of their walls. Peter Dietz, the founder of Social Actions, an open source database of actions anyone can take for social change efforts, said, "Collaborative dynamics and processes can be far more effective at producing innovation than competition [can]."[7]

Netflix, the movie rental company, sponsored a competition with a prize of $1 million. Netflix recommends movies to their customers online using a complex algorithm based on the previous viewing choices of that customer and comparing it to others. The winning person or organization would improve the percentage of movies recommended to their customers that they would then watch and love by 10 percent. *The New York Times* reported one surprising finding at the conclusion: "The biggest lesson learned, according to members of the two top teams, was the power of collaboration."[8]

The top two groups were collaborations of people and organizations that could have viewed one another as competitors. Instead, they realized their best chance of winning was for each person or organization to focus on what they did best and create a team of people with the other skills needed to win the prize.

Let's help an organization practice moving from scarcity to abundance. An executive director told us a few months ago she needed to raise $30,000 for a new Web site. Using her scarcity lens, she thought the only solution to her problem was to compete with many other organizations for a grant to underwrite the project from a limited number of foundations.

We helped her reframe the issue using an abundance lens. She didn't need $30,000; she needed a new Web site. Certainly, she could get a new Web site if she applied for a grant, asked a donor for the funds, or approached a Web development company for pro bono assistance. But these aren't the only ways. She could also post a question on one of her social media channels asking who can help create a new Web site. Imagine the creative responses: Maybe someone wants to hone her Web development skills and add this effort to her résumé. Or maybe professionals can barter their skills, with a Web developer tackling the site in return for a tutorial in proposal writing.

Her options show that simplicity is more than a mind-set for organizations. It also means choosing *not* to do some things merely because "that's the way they've always been done."

SIMPLIFYING YOUR ORGANIZATION

It is essential that nonprofit organizations focus on developing the simplest ideas, structures, and processes possible. In *The Power of Less*, Leo Babauta defines simplicity as a two-step process: identify the essential elements of what you do, and then eliminate the rest. We offer a modification of this adage to fit the particular needs of social change organizations: *Do what you do best and network the rest.*[9]

Eugene Eric Kim, an expert in online collaboration, says simplicity is the key to scaling social change efforts. "Think about ants," he says. "They do two things really well: haul things and leave trails. This is the key to working in a networked way . . . focusing on one or two things that are done really well. That's the only way to scale."[10]

Ward Cunningham, the celebrated computer programmer and creator of the wiki tool, said, "Simplicity is the shortest path to a solution. You are always taught to do as much as you can. Always put checks in. Always look for exceptions. Always handle the most general case. Always give the user the best advice. Always print a meaningful error message. Always this. Always that. You have so many things in the background that you're supposed to do, there's no room left to think. I say, forget all that and ask yourself, "What's the simplest thing that could possibly work?"[11]

So, where and how can organizations begin to become simpler? Here are a few suggestions:

Have a heart-to-heart with yourself. People can fall in love with their own programs. Once you've invested in its development, raised money for it, and willed it along year after year, letting it go can break your heart. But almost every organization has programs, services, and efforts that go on mainly because they always have, not because they are still needed or effective. It is imperative for organizations to get down to the fundamentals of who they are and what they do best, and to let go of the rest. The goal is to do the fewest, not the most, things well to meet the organization's mission.

Leverage the network. Once it becomes clear what constitutes the core of an organization's efforts, then it's time to leverage the network for the rest. In his book *Trust Agents*, Chris Brogan calls this the Archimedes Principle. He writes, "Give me a lever long enough and I'll move the world. Understanding leverage, especially the human kind, is vital to developing your abilities in this space."[12]

When we ask staffers what their networks suggested when they were asked for advice, they often admit it never occurred to them to ask. As we discuss in Chapter Five, "Listening, Engaging, and Building Relationships," their reticence comes from a reluctance to look weak or indecisive to outside people. Healthy networks require oxygen, or conversations, to grow, and parts of these conversations are requests for help.

Organizations will find people and other organizations with good ideas and an interest in working together. This is the leverage that they need to stop doing everything alone while still ensuring that a lot is getting done in the ecosystem. All these organizations and people are right there, in the network, on LinkedIn and Facebook and Twitter, waiting to connect with and support an organization's efforts.

Networking the rest is not the same as developing cumbersome institutional collaborations sealed by contract. Formal, contractual relationships are part of the complexity of organizational life that slows everything down; it requires oversight and deliverables and is usually undergirded by a healthy dose of suspicion.

Of course, there are times when contracts are necessary, particularly to safeguard client confidentiality. But too often, partnerships turn into contractual obligations only because of an organizational default setting, not out of necessity. Leveraging the network means clarifying roles, coordinating efforts, keeping apprised of what one another is doing, and sharing resources and ideas.

One additional benefit of leveraging is that networks naturally have redundancies built into them. In a formal contractual relationship, an organization would be locked into one or two other organizations. Leveraging enables an organization to work with many organizations and people, safeguarding against the problem of leaning too heavily on one person or organization to do something. And there are no long-term obligations to continue to work with any particular group.

Leveraging a network enables a staff of two to have a staff of, say, twenty working on its behalf. What's more, that staff of two isn't working fourteen hours a day doing everything alone. David Venn, a communications professional in the field of adolescent mental health, experienced this shift firsthand: "We've used social networks to connect with other organizations so we don't have to do all the heavy lifting. We're able to accomplish much more than by operating as [an] organizational island. We are able to focus on what we know best—youth mental health."[13]

Simplify processes using social media. Organizations need to question their internal processes and systems to ensure they are as friction-free as possible. For instance, organizations spend enormous amounts of time scheduling meetings.

They can reduce scheduling time using free Web-based tools like Meeting Wizard and Doodle. Skype is a free telecommunications system for videoconferencing that can substitute for in-person meetings. Google documents, wikis such as PBWiki, and Yahoo! and Google Groups are all free tools that support and coordinate group work. Users of these tools can store documents, create and share project schedules, and build an e-mail listserv for projects.

Reimagine productivity. Incorporating social media into organizational life challenges the underlying assumptions that senior managers have about work and productivity. If one measures productivity solely as an efficiency standard or a checklist of tasks completed, then staffers engaging with social media will fail the test. Defining productivity for social media use looks and feels different from traditional ways of working. Advancing the organization's mission by building a network of supporters who will help some time in the future in myriad and unexpected ways means spending time in conversations that may not have any immediate outcomes.

Simplifying organizational processes is helpful, but it won't completely eliminate the dark shadow that hovers over organizations—staffers' overwhelming feeling that they are drowning in their work. They feel this way because it is true.

DOING MORE BY DOING LESS

When we discuss using social media with nonprofit staffers, they often pale at the thought of adding one more thing to their to-do list. As if that were possible! But social media are not another thing to do. Using social media is a way of working that has to be woven into an organization's fabric and an individual's work flow. But first, we have to pare down what we do because our connected, social world presents far more opportunities than ever for distraction.

"Overwhelming" captures how it feels to be connected to so many people and information sources at once. Even those of us happily swirling in the midst of the social media maelstrom feel we are drowning in information, content, links, e-mails, blog posts, tweets, and friend updates. We are quickly losing our ability to concentrate on one thing at a time in this multitasking, beeping, buzzing world.

Paul Lamb, a nonprofit consultant, writes, "The capacity of humans to productively focus on more than one task at a time degrades significantly after two tasks are introduced simultaneously. We can talk on the cell phone while driving, but by adding a third activity—say putting on makeup—reaction times diminish to the equivalent of driving drunk."[14]

The social media pioneer Howard Rheingold found that the students in his course at the University of California at Berkeley actually had to practice shutting down their laptops to concentrate on the conversation at hand. "Attention," he writes, "is a skill that must be learned, shaped, practiced; this skill must evolve if we are to evolve."[15]

The challenge, therefore, is to figure out what to use when and how so we can better manage a world with social media in it.

Larry Blumenthal, director of social media strategy for The Robert Wood Johnson Foundation, reflected on a staff person's efforts to build social media into their work: "If we can get past the idea that social media is just one more thing to do, one more thing to learn, we will see that these tools can help us do what we are already doing—only more effectively."[16] Using social media well simplifies our work. Here are some strategies for simplifying one's work life with social media:

- **Create a schedule**. Spending endless hours wandering around Facebook and Twitter is not sustainable—at least, not for people who don't live in a college dorm room. Set a time limit—say, an hour a day—for checking these kinds of social sites. Put a sticky note on your computer or desk, and keep a tally of how long you spend on various social media channels online. Patterns will develop after a week of monitoring your social media usage. Think about how valuable your time is and how that matches with how you are spending it online. Then create a schedule of what you want to check, when, and for how long. Maybe 8 to 9 A.M. is the time to check e-mail, and 1 to 2 P.M. is the time to check Twitter and Facebook.

- **Take advantage of Google**. Google has an amazing array of free tools and mechanisms for putting you in charge of your own slice of the Web. For instance, setting up your own Google Alerts puts the Google search engine to work for you searching the Web for news and blog posts according to your keywords and delivers them to you. You set the parameters of what you want to know about and Google sends the information into your in-box.

- **Prune your information flow**. Speaking of your in-box, it is important that you take charge of it, not the other way around. Unsubscribe to nonessential newsletters and lists. Schedule your Google Alerts to come in once a week rather than once a day. Reduce the number of news sites and blogs on your **Google Reader** or home page. Delete e-mails that have been sitting in your in-box for longer than you can remember. Pare down your information flow to the critical information and news you need to be effective and creative in your work. Just be careful not to put up so many filters and walls that someone would need a catapult to share with you an interesting idea or article or person.

• **Choose your go-to tools carefully**. We have discussed the need for everyone to become comfortable and facile using a variety of social media tools. That does not mean that everyone has to use every tool all the time. Focus on using the tools that work best for you. Practice on the channels that fit your style and interests, and resonate more with your network. Focus your time on using those tools.

• **Find your trusted sources**. As discussed in Chapter Four, "Creating a Social Culture," finding trusted sources of information shortens the time you have to spend looking for it. Identify five to ten trusted bloggers to ensure your attention is well used when reading those blogs. The same trusted source notion applies to Twitter, Facebook, and MySpace. Sometimes a trusted source to follow online is someone you know personally or who is a topical expert.

• **Become a better friend**. When online social networking sites began, the tendency of many people was to collect up friends like prizes at a fair. But it can become overwhelming to use channels like Facebook with too many voices in the mix. Your collection of friends on Twitter and Facebook may have happened by happenstance, but it doesn't have to stay that way. Slim down your friend lists to essential people. You will be able to hear their voices and be a better friend to them in return.

Filter the conversation. Learn how to use the myriad filters and tools on channels like Facebook to better organize the conversations. Organize your Twitter stream to highlight messages from favorite people. It is important to become intentional about the messages you allow to take up your time. Use the available tools to make information streams more manageable.

• **Turn the darn computer off and go for a walk!** Staring at a monitor with its reflected lights dancing on your retinas is de-energizing after a while. These moments intensify the effects of information overload. Get up and take a walk or move around. Also, feel free to take a break from a particular social media tool for a while. This will be a chance to evaluate whether that tool is really useful to you.

When the effects of simplicity and lighter individual workloads come together, organizations can accomplish much more than they ever could before. One small arts organization in Vermont demonstrates how this is possible.

SIMPLY RIVER ARTS IN VERMONT

River Arts was started in 1999 to serve the Lamoille Valley in the rural communities of northern Vermont. The organization emerged from a series of community conversations that highlighted the dearth of opportunities to learn about and participate in the visual and performing arts locally.

River Arts provides a broad array of performing and visual art programs. It hosts weekly arts workshops for children and adults, sponsors concerts and festivals, manages a gallery, and hosts an artist-in-residence. Over the course of a year, the organization serves four hundred to five hundred people through their workshops. It serves another two hundred children at a summer camp.

By traditional standards, River Arts is a tiny organization with an annual budget of less than $200,000 and a staff of three people. But those are the wrong measures to use for River Arts. It is, in fact, an enormous network of people and organizations that is bringing performing and visual arts to a formerly underserved part of Vermont—and having a tremendous impact on the community as a result.

Steve Ames was hired as River Arts' program director, the organization's first employee, in 2002 and soon became executive director. Steve thinks of the organization more as a community center that focuses on the arts rather than as an arts organization. The best way for the organization to engage other people, he believes, is to follow what they want to do rather than prescribe what and how the arts should be practiced.[17]

Steve also ardently believes in and practices organizational simplicity. He says, "If we can simplify, we can do more with our time that's mission-related. If we can do payroll, promotion, rental, communications, etc., more simply, then we can do more programming . . . and we can solve people's problems more quickly."[18]

One way the organization simplifies its efforts is by embracing social media. Steve was an early adopter of Facebook, which River Arts uses to plan events in lieu of placing expensive advertisements in the local paper. They have an e-mail list of 1,600 people and use their Web site to engage in conversations, with all staffers sharing responsibility for blogging.

But simplicity is as much a mind-set as a process for River Arts. The organization is not trying to be perfect, according to Steve, nor is it interested in owning every arts effort in the region. The organization thinks of itself as a catalyst rather than a producer of programs and events.

For example, a few years ago, River Arts put on its big annual art show. The show took an enormous amount of work and fundraising to produce. After a few years, another organization in the region began a similar event. Rather than view the newcomer as unwelcome competition, River Arts decided to let their event go.

Similarly, River Arts identifies talented artists and asks them about their passion to find out what they might want to teach. The organization has found this engages energetic teachers who electrify their students. It also leverages resources in their network who might otherwise not be interested in teaching a prescribed curriculum.

River Arts pares down its efforts internally to the essentials. It uses social media when possible to connect and engage with people. The organization lets go of efforts others can do as well as or better than they can. And they follow their community's passion rather than developing all strategies on their own. Altogether, River Arts is a simple and effective Networked Nonprofit.

CONCLUSION

Simplicity is more than an economic equation, more than a tactic for hard financial times. It is, simply, a better way for social change organizations to accomplish more with fewer financial resources.

Simplicity requires organizations to decouple themselves from the assumption that by doing more they are automatically better able to meet their missions. Doing more just means being busier. It takes courage for organizations and their people to stop doing what they've always done. It means letting go of efforts, like River Arts did, and letting someone else take the credit. It means rethinking the definition of success as something other than constant growth in budget and staff. Only then will people and organizations have the room to breathe, think, and succeed.

Twenty Questions for Simplifying Your Workload

Addressing your information overload simplifies and lightens your individual workload. Information overload is really about how you feel about information. If you answer yes to more than five of these questions, it's time to make some changes.

- When you open your e-mail client, does it make you feel anxious about the work that you don't have time to do?
- Do you open your e-mail in the morning before making a prioritized to-do list, and several hours later forget what it was in the first place you wanted to accomplish today?
- Do you frequently forget information you need to know?
- Do you ever wish the Web or social media would just go away?
- Do you have e-mail messages sitting in your inbox for more than six months that are "pending" further action or unread?
- Do you sometimes wish you could read or type faster?
- Do you experience frustration at the amount of electronic information you need to process daily?
- Do you sit at your computer for longer than an hour at a time without getting up to take a break?
- Do you constantly check (even in the bathroom) your e-mail, Twitter, or other online service because you are afraid that if you don't, you will become so far behind that you will never catch up?
- Is the only time you're offline when you are sleeping?
- Do you feel that you often cannot concentrate?
- Are you subscribed to so many blogs that you can't read them all and it makes you feel bad?
- Do you feel that you have to read word for word all information that comes into your e-mail box, RSS reader, or Twitter?
- Are you always seeking out additional information from the Internet or friends online to support a decision or complete a project, but never processing it all?
- Do you get anxious if you are away from the Internet for too long?
- Do you open up multiple tabs in your browser and then forget what you were going to do?
- Is your e-mail, Google documents, or hard drive filled with "virtual piles" of information or "drafts" that haven't been processed?

- Are you afraid to delete e-mail or old files because you just might need them someday?
- Are you unable to locate electronic documents, blog posts, e-mail messages, or other online information that you need at the moment without wasting time playing "find the file"?
- Do you find yourself easily distracted by online resources that allow you to avoid other, pending work?

REFLECTION QUESTIONS

Organizational Simplicity

- How risk-averse is your organization?
- What factors create complexity in your organization's programs?
- How much of the complexity in your organization is self-inflicted?
- How do tried-and-true solutions actually increase complexity in your organization?
- How do you know you're stuck in scarcity thinking mode?
- Does your organization have difficulty letting go of programs? Why?
- What are the elements of a new business model that will allow your organization to fully embrace radical simplicity?

Avoiding Information Overload

- How do you make value judgments on the information that comes to you via your e-mail box or RSS reader?
- How effective are your personal information filing systems and sharing methods for electronic information? What works? What doesn't? Why?
- What are some coping strategies that you use to deal with the stress of information overload?
- How could the use of technology help you avoid information overload, rather than cause it?

PART TWO

What to Do as a Networked Nonprofit

If you don't think that small things can make a big difference, you've never slept in a bed with a mosquito!

—Arianna Huffington

Working with Crowds

The Brooklyn Museum launched a photography exhibition in 2008 called the "Changing Faces of Brooklyn." But it wasn't just an ordinary exhibit; rather, it was an experiment in engaging the public as an integral part of creating the exhibition. The Museum called the experiment "Click! A Crowd-Curated Exhibition."

The public was invited to take part in the exhibition as participants and curators. The Brooklyn Museum's open call for photographs netted 389 entries uploaded to the museum's Web site. The public was then invited to rank the images for inclusion in the show. Much to the museum's delight, over 3000 people—3,344 to be exact—participated in the review process.[1]

"Click! A Crowd-Curated Exhibition" culminated in an in-person show at the Museum. The photographs were installed according to their relative ranking from the public review process.

Eugenie Tsai, the Brooklyn Museum's John and Barbara Vogelstein Curator of Contemporary Art, reflected, "What struck me was that the average amount of time that people looked at the image was twenty-two seconds. There are studies of museum visitors that show on average, most people look at a work of art for six seconds."[2]

The museum's Web site continues to provide interesting opportunities for the public to view the images. For instance, viewers can see how self-described experts ranked them or how novices ranked them, providing quite different perspectives of what each group valued. The museum also made available the data collected from the reviewers for analysis by art experts in online communities.

"Click! A Crowd-Curated Exhibition" accomplished a great deal at very little cost for the museum. It empowered the audience to contribute to the creation of the exhibit without feeling that a degree in art history was necessary. It also enabled the museum to weave itself directly into its own community's fabric, since a majority of the online reviewers were local residents. Most important, it helped to take down the walls between the museum as an institution and its public.

The exhibition was the brainchild of Shelley Bernstein, the head of the information technologies department for the museum. She said, "The entire exhibition is based on the participation of the community, both in the open call and in the evaluation stage, so the exhibition's contents are entirely up to the community. We are just providing the container, the mechanism so it can function."[3]

Shelley and her colleagues based the exhibition on the concepts articulated by Jeff Howe in his book *Crowdsourcing—Why the Power of the Crowd Is Driving the Future of Business*. **Crowdsourcing** is the process of organizing many people to participate in a joint project, often in small ways. The results are greater than an individual or organization could have accomplished alone.

Of course, collective activities are not new to social media. For instance, on a cold December day in 1900, the Audubon Society organized the first Christmas Bird Count to catalogue all the birds of the Western Hemisphere. But using social media enables the Society to increase this activity with less effort and less cost. A century after its inception, over 52,000 people in 1,823 places across 17 countries participated in the Christmas Bird Count. They receive their instructions via e-mail and input their data directly into the Audubon Society's Web site.

Using social media to build and strengthen crowds and spread out an organization's work is one of the most powerful reasons to work as a networked nonprofit. Amanda Rose, one of the architects of the worldwide fundraising effort called Twestival, explains: "In some cases it can be more work . . . but we absolutely couldn't do it alone. Crowds are powerful. *But* you must know how to effectively use them or it can definitely be more work to manage them."[4]

This chapter will describe the different activities crowds can undertake, explain how to break efforts down into bite-size pieces, and discuss how to engage crowds in an iterative process of planning and implementation we call *microplanning.*

THE DIFFERENT KINDS OF CROWDSOURCING

Crowds come in all different sizes and shapes. There is no one right way to use crowdsourcing; conversely, organizations may use a combination of crowdsourcing efforts to meet their needs. Social media tools for capturing the work of crowds include wikis and other group work spaces such as Google or Yahoo! Groups. Web sites with rating systems are useful for voting efforts, and of course, blogs can provide updates and reflections on crowdsourcing efforts as they unfold.

Crowdsourcing can be classified into four categories, each with a specific goal.

- **Collective intelligence or crowd wisdom.** A group of individuals has more knowledge for solving a problem than any single individual. Collective intelligence creates a "cloud" of information that many people can distribute for use. The Audubon Society's Christmas Bird Count is an example of collective intelligence. Some data can also be "mashed up" or made available for a variety of uses. Everyblock Chicago is a Web site with a mash-up of data. Users can organize and use the data by police beat, neighborhood, ward, ZIP code, date, or type of crime for their own purposes.

- **Crowd creation.** Crowds can create original works of knowledge or art. The Royal Opera used Twitter to crowdsource a new opera in the summer of 2009. The opera company encouraged Twitter users to send suggestions for the plot to the organization's Twitter address. The opera staff collected the suggestions and summarized them on their blog. The musical director also blogged about the emerging, nonlinear story line and how it would be merged with original music composed by Helen Porter. The company performed the opera in September 2009 as part of a three-day festival sponsored by Deloitte to celebrate innovation in the arts.[5]

Opera is not the only art form that has experimented with crowdsourcing. Twitter Community Choreography is an ongoing experiment of the Dance Theater Workshop. Each week it asks its Twitter followers to contribute to one movement. The Dance Theater Workshop then performs that movement and posts a video of it on YouTube.

- **Crowd voting.** Crowds love to vote on their favorite things like ideas, artwork, essays, and people. The Internet lends itself to voting, making the votes easy to see and share and the results instantaneous. Organizations can take polls on the temperature of a crowd and see what they like and don't like. TechSoup Global sponsors an annual event, NetSquared, which asks its crowd to vote online for the best applications of social media for social change. Winners receive a cash prize and other resources.

- **Crowd funding**. This category taps the collective pocketbook, encouraging groups to fund an effort that benefits many people. Contributions can be a donation or a purchase, but with no expectation that the funds will be repaid. The idea is to leverage the funds of the crowd to complete a project they support. For example, the Web site www.Spot.Us raises money from the public to commission journalists to work on investigative stories.

By using these kinds of crowdsourcing techniques, groups of people can work in concert (and in the Royal Opera's case, literally, in concert!) toward a common goal. But successful crowdsourcing doesn't just happen. The inflection between the enormous supply of people willing to help and the real needs of organizations must be carefully, strategically traversed. Organizations must figure out how to break their work down into bite-size pieces for their crowd to succeed and so they themselves can benefit from the work.

MAKING PROJECTS BITE-SIZE

Working with crowds takes some practice for most organizations but as Katya Andresen wrote, ". . . small steps are more likely to add up to a big change than are ambitious calls to action."[6] It is the responsibility of organizations to make sure that the bite-size pieces with which crowds engage fit into a larger, strategic mosaic for change. Otherwise they run the risk of "slactivism."

According to the online Urban Dictionary, *slactivism* is "the act of participating in obviously pointless activities as an expedient alternative to actually expending effort to fix a problem." Developing clear strategies for working with crowds is not only the best route to problem solving but it also honors the work of the crowds and keeps them from wasting time on busywork.

Organizations should ask and answer three questions when preparing to work with crowds:

- **What should the crowd do?** Organizations must clearly think through what they want their crowds to do at the outset of an effort. In a dilemma reminiscent of Goldilocks, if the tasks are too global they will seem overwhelming and people won't participate. But if the tasks are too granular, they will not interest the group. It will require experimentation and a lot of input from the organization's network to identify ways to break up the work into doable, interesting, modular pieces.

- **Who needs to be included in this crowd?** Not just any crowd will do for every effort. It is important to connect with the *right* crowd. An organization has to decide if it needs particular expertise for a project or whether enthusiasm and interest will suffice. Identifying people with particular skills is what excellent network weavers do as part of their everyday work. The weavers can help recruit participants by explaining what skills and knowledge are needed and why the project matters. Keep in mind that targeting specific kinds of expertise doesn't exclude others from participating.

- **What will we do with the crowd's input?** Organizations make two common mistakes when working with crowds. The first mistake is not being forthright about what they will do with the input they receive from their crowd. What happens to the suggestions that are put into the online suggestion box? Will an internal committee review the suggestions and choose which ones to accept? Will they be reviewed by the CEO and not necessarily acted on, but used to provide context for the organization's work? To avoid this, organizations must decide early on exactly how they will use the crowd's input, advice, data, and expertise, and then communicate that clearly.

The second mistake organizations make is assuming they have to accept all of the crowd's input without question or disagreement. When organizations assume their role is to sit back and let the crowds operate alone, it is easy to end up resenting or ignoring the results. When organizations value input and participate in efforts with crowds in open and honest ways—two cornerstones of transparency—they can disagree with the direction the crowd is going in without usurping or diluting its efforts. Participants will feel like full partners, not window dressing, when organizations treat them as adults. Crowds don't mind disagreement; they do mind deception.

Once organizations decide these questions about their crowdsourcing (perhaps with the help of outsiders), the implementation process we call *microplanning* begins.

MICROPLANNING WITH CROWDS

When Fortresses plan campaigns with expensive, closed, time-consuming processes, the results often feel unwieldy and risky. To avoid risk, these organizations spend even more energy trying to mitigate it. This paralyzing, terrified way of working distances organizations from their communities, reducing their chance of success as it traps them in a vicious cycle.

Clay Shirky, the author of *Here Comes Everybody*, said, "We spend so much time trying to make something perfect rather than just trying something." Microplanning provides an alternative for organizations from the oppressive cost and risk associated with big campaigns. Microplanning is an iterative process of small experiments that lets organizations change, scale, or scrap them easily, quickly, and inexpensively.

Microplanning has several benefits, including

- Creating buy-in for efforts sooner by including larger numbers of people in an unfolding implementation process
- Unhooking organizations from needing all of the answers before they can get started
- Reducing risk by focusing on short, strategic bursts of activity that can be altered in real time and scaled without huge financial expenditures

Microplanning particularly applies to programs, communications, marketing, and fundraising. It takes on the popular notion that nonprofit campaigns must be completely organized before engaging outside people. Instead of relying on big, expensive campaigns that go through exhausting boom and bust cycles, organizations can inch their way into efforts, significantly reducing their risk and saving their energy.

Engaging in microplanning is not the same thing as being unplanned. Organizations still need planning tools such as logic models and theories of change to identify goals and results. But microplanning enables them to start more easily, leaving the plans open and unsealed for crowds to help shape and manage over time.

It might seem incongruous that an organization needs to develop clear goals while at the same time opening itself up to the crowd's wisdom and guidance. But clear goals and outcomes give the community a framework to work within as they shape specific processes and activities. And participation by crowds enables an organization to spread out the responsibility and increase the public buy-in for efforts.

Microplanning is philosophically similar to other participatory processes that have dotted the nonprofit landscape for years. Participatory program planning and evaluation efforts are popular ways of incorporating more voices into program and evaluation plans. Community development efforts have often included design charrettes to elicit input from larger community segments. Microplanning builds on these concepts by adding the power of social media, thereby inexpensively extending and deepening participation over longer periods of time.

Microplanning can discomfort staff people who feel they have a tried-and-true methodology for implementing work. After all, organizations often hire staffers for their expertise, which means they have a very good idea of what strategies work for which projects. Rather than silo this knowledge, however, staff should share those strategies with the community and show they are open to suggestions on how to make them even better.

Microplanning can help develop new services or refine old ones. It can narrow down advocacy efforts, or decide if there even should be an advocacy effort. Crowds can help develop new fundraising ideas, find resources that can be donated, advertise the event, and connect with terrific speakers. No matter what the details are, the conversation about an event or program unfolds over time and becomes part of the effort itself.

THE HUDSON INSTITUTE LEARNS TO MICROPLAN

The Hudson Institute's The Center for Global Prosperity raises awareness of the private sector's central role in creating economic growth and prosperity around the world. The Center's core product is the annual Index of Global Philanthropy and Remittances, which details the sources and magnitude of private giving to the developing world. The organization based the Index on traditional research techniques such as literature reviews, interviews, and surveys.

During the summer of 2008, Carol Adelman, the Center's director, began a conversation among a small team of research fellows, senior researchers, interns, and project managers to explore ways the Center could integrate social media into its work. The group first thought of creating a Facebook page to distribute the Index. But with the help of an outside consultant, they realized that putting up a Facebook page to push out the Index before building relationships online would probably not succeed.

These discussions also created an opportunity for the Center to free itself from the notion that it could only turn to traditional research sources for Index data, particularly related to young people and giving. Engaging in more places online, with many people in many different places, would help shape future iterations of the Index. Microplanning seemed a better way to go.

Carol and her group articulated their goals for microplanning the Index. They included

- Identifying examples, stories, and trends of global philanthropy from sources such as blogs, Facebook, and Twitter to support the Center's research
- Getting a deeper understanding about "younger generations" and their attitudes, motivations, and activities around philanthropy
- Identifying and engaging with philanthropy bloggers to discuss the Index

Carol's group identified keywords and prepared to start listening on social media channels including Twitter and Facebook. But they quickly hit a roadblock when older staff members expressed their discomfort with younger staff members going online and representing the Center in what they felt were unsupervised ways.

Instead of giving up the idea, the Center staff took the opportunity to discuss their feelings about being open to the public online. These conversations helped the Center shift its focus outward. It also showed older staff members the urgency in moving away from one-way monologues to two-way conversations about their research with people beyond their walls.

Together, staff members identified a work flow that let senior research fellows effectively oversee and manage junior staffers' work on social network sites. What's more, working with the junior staff this way also helped the senior staff become more facile and comfortable with social media.

Once the senior staff members reached their comfort level, younger staffers such as Yulya Spantchak, a research and communications associate, began to listen online. Yulya monitored blogs focused on philanthropy, global giving, nonprofit work, corporate social responsibility, and other related topics identified by the team. Each week, she summarized the news and topics that people in the field were blogging about and analyzed those blogs' comments. In addition, the Center established a Twitter profile to identify potential case studies, share information, and talk to more people about their work. The Center staff also created individual profiles on Facebook to track conversations taking place on different group pages and Fan pages related to their research topics.

Organically over six months, the Center's work changed. They were listening and talking to people on many channels, including using an RSS reader to scan the Web for relevant blog posts, and finding and interviewing young people on Facebook as part of the Index data collection. They developed case studies for the annual report that involved more young people, and they discovered new avenues for sharing results with people they weren't reaching before. In this way, the Index became less of a product and more of a process of learning and engagement with many people across the Web.

Another byproduct of their microplanning effort: the Center's staff developed a greater appreciation, comfort level, and facility with using social media. Most important, they learned how to integrate working in a different way into their daily routines. As Carol Adelman recalled in retrospect, "The most important point was linking the use of social media to our work flow, being consistent, and getting comfortable."[7]

CROWDSOURCING CAUTIONS

Working with crowds is not a cure-all for every effort. Just as staffers alone aren't always the best problem solvers, crowds are not always the best problem solvers either. In order to be realistic about crowdsourcing, organizations should be aware of its potential downsides, which include the following:

• **Crowds are unpredictable**. It is impossible to predict when and why crowds will show up. This can be frustrating, but it simply reflects real life online. People come and go as they please, not as organizations want them to. Organizations must maintain their equilibrium when their crowds are not engaged or staying home. Keep talking with the network, build relationships, continue to toss out ideas, and listen to what people have to say. Crowds aren't shy; when an issue or task strikes their fancy, they'll be there in large numbers.

• **Crowds can become angry mobs**. When angered, crowds can become mobs and use their collective power to punish organizations and people. McNeal Consumer Healthcare, the company that makes the pain reliever Motrin, was faced with an angry online crowd in November 2008. The company posted what it considered a friendly and empathetic video about the pain mothers feel carrying their babies in slings—pain that Motrin could reduce. The narrator for the ad said that wearing a baby in a sling was "in fashion," which some women found patronizing. But the two sentences that followed sent the mob into a frenzy: "Plus, it totally makes me look like an official mom. And so if I look tired and crazy, people will understand why."

One crucial, unwritten rule of motherhood is that only mothers can call themselves "tired" and "crazy." Others—particularly faceless companies and their ad agencies—shouldn't dare. Within hours a large number of mommy bloggers were in full-throated outrage. The subject quickly became one of the hottest trends on Twitter. And while the storm built, McNeal and their advertising firm slept, letting an entire weekend pass by without listening and hearing what was going on. By Monday, a full-fledged online hurricane was under way. The company quickly pulled the ad and apologized, but the angry crowd had had its say. Nonprofit organizations can also organize their own mobs. People for the Ethical Treatment of Animals (PETA) protested the use of fur by the online shoe store Zappos. They expressed their outrage primarily through Twitter, sending over eleven thousand protest messages to Zappos's Twitter account in just a few days. Zappos quickly enacted a policy never to sell products containing animal fur.

Not all mobs are necessarily angry. Using their Web site and other communication channels, Carrotmob organizes consumers to buy from socially responsible businesses as a reward for their commitment to improving the world. The model is similar to a buycott, the opposite of a boycott.

In the first-ever Carrotmob event, a liquor store agreed to invest in upgrades that made the building more energy efficient. In exchange, hundreds of Carrotmobbers showed up all at once to support the winning liquor store.[8]

• **Crowd contributions are 90 percent useless**. Research on crowdsourcing found that the overwhelming majority of crowdsourced efforts were not useful, an outcome termed Sturgeon's Law.[9] So why go through all this trouble if 90 percent of the output will be terrible? Because any process of developing ideas, knowledge, and new products—whether online or on land—requires wading through mistakes and missteps before getting any traction. And because the exercise of being creative and contributing to something, even if it isn't ultimately useful, is crucial for building relationships with people and helping them flex their own creativity and talents. And finally, because the 10 percent that *is* good is really worth it.

• **Crowds and organizations may be done**. Unlike traditional efforts on land that seemingly go on forever, online crowds can finish their work. Once the work is done, or more likely has fizzled, there is nothing wrong with winding down the effort. This is in keeping with the notion of organizational simplicity. There may even be times when organizations and their crowds have a disagreement that requires either the project, or part of the crowd, to go away. Again, there is nothing wrong with these shifts as long as the organization sticks to its principles of transparency and communicates openly and often about what is happening and why.

CONCLUSION

Some critics may sneer at what they believe to be amateurs bumbling around in territory formerly the reserve of professionals. And organizations are still ultimately responsible for how their efforts unfold.

But at its best, crowdsourcing is a marriage between professionals and volunteers who have the goodwill and passion to work together to benefit an entire community. Leveraging crowds is an important and inexpensive way to lift the oppressive weight that so many staffers feel on their shoulders. And by microplanning, organizations can reduce the risk and fear that traditional planning processes create and enable more people to participate in more meaningful ways for social change.

The Magic Tweet: Crowdsourcing Opera Analysis

The Royal Opera House announced its intention of working with its crowd on Twitter to create the story line for a brand-new opera, 140 characters at a time. They told their audience they were exploring how short, 140-character contributions can build upon each other to create a nonlinear narrative—like a "Choose Your Own Adventure" story or a game of Consequences.

The company gave a brief context for the story and then encouraged their followers on Twitter to tweet opera lines. Meanwhile, the opera director regularly blogged with updates on the story, and offered his thoughts on how the story could combine with music, acting, and singing to become a finished piece.

The Royal Opera House encouraged people to contribute, but did not necessarily use all the lines they received. They were careful to recognize each person's contribution.

When the opera was complete, they reported back and shared the finished product.

Not surprisingly, the opera was sold out.

Note: Figures 8.1–8.5 on the following pages show some of the Twitter communications during this process.

(Continued)

Figure 8.1
Royal Opera House Invites Audience to Participate

@Ikviakninoff add your line of the story by tweeting to #youropera and see the latest story by searching youropera. Updating the blog now.

3:57 AM Aug 18th from web in reply to Ikviakninoff

youropera
DeloitteIgniteOpera

Figure 8.2
Royal Opera House Keeps Encouraging Audience to Tweet Opera Lines

Last day of the opera proper today. Can you tweet the last line? Then pls can ppl craft pithy 1-act encore pieces so we end w/a song&dance!

10:44 AM Aug 25th from web

youropera
DeloitteIgniteOpera

**Figure 8.3
Royal Opera House Recognizes Each Contribution,
Even If Not Used in Opera**

twitter

@MiniVanDents even if your tweets didn't make it in word for word, you helped make the first part of the story - who knows where it will go!

4:15 AM Sep 5th from Tweetie in reply to MiniVanDents

 youropera
DeloitteIgniteOpera

**Figure 8.4
Royal Opera House Shares Progress of Rehearsals**

twitter

Just seen the amazing first #youropera rehearsal. Much behind-the-scenes work from the fabulous creative team. Sneak preview coming soon!

12:55 PM Sep 2nd from web

 youropera
DeloitteIgniteOpera

(Continued)

Figure 8.5
Royal Opera House Sells Out Opera

And it's a full house! #youropera
http://yfrog.com/588d7gj

11:15 AM Sep 5th from Tweetie

youropera
DeloitteIgniteOpera

Source: All the figures are reprinted with the permission of the Royal Opera House, London. Adapted from Beth Kanter, Beth's Blog, August 2009, **http://beth.typepad .com/beths_blog/2009/08/the-magic-tweet-crowdsourcing-an-opera-on-twitter-.html** (accessed on February 18, 2010).

Crowdsourcing Do's and Don'ts

Do's

- Have a clear objective and metric on the front end, but try to avoid over-planning or overproducing your strategies.
- Leave room to tweak or adjust your content or messaging based on what you hear through listening.
- Have shorter, more frequent meetings to make decisions in real time as you implement strategy.
- Document your results along the way (quantitative and qualitative) and leave some time for reflection.
- Have faith in your network or community—they will respond if you have built it in the right way.
- Reward people publicly for their participation and feedback.
- Be prepared—not every contribution will be stunning or of high quality, but with careful facilitation you can keep everyone engaged.

Don'ts

- Avoid thinking you need to do more research to make the decision. Adopt a "try it, fix it" attitude.

- Don't expect to get it right the first time or even the second time. Making mistakes and failing is part of the process—learn from it.

- Crowds can't be trained like seals, but they can be guided.

- Don't overstructure or overthink the tasks. Have faith in the crowds.

REFLECTION QUESTIONS

- What do you want to accomplish with crowdsourcing? What's your goal?

- What model of crowdsourcing will help you reach your goal?

- Who will guide the crowd? Managing crowds is not a full-time job, but it may need full-time attention for a few days at a time. The skills needed are listening, summarizing, and the ability to swim through unstructured data.

- What crowd do you want to reach? How will you invite them to participate?

- Do you need incentives for participation?

- Do you know what will keep the crowd motivated?

Learning Loops

The images were gruesome and searing. The repeated television and YouTube clips sickened and outraged people around the world. Blogs and newspapers lit up with reactions.

The images depicted pit bull terrier dogs trained to viciously fight one another for sport, with the losers often drowned or electrocuted. By itself a dog-fighting ring story might not have garnered attention. But this story was huge news because Michael Vick, a star quarterback in the National Football League, had financed and housed the operation.

Enter The Humane Society of the United States, founded in 1954 to celebrate animals and protect them from cruelty. If the Michael Vick story had broken in 1977 rather than 2007, the organization would likely have responded with a press release condemning Michael Vick and his coconspirators, and followed it with a direct-mail fundraising letter asking supporters for $10, $15, or $25 to support the Humane Society. But that was then, before bloggers and tweeters, Facebook and YouTube—before millions of people had their own means for sharing their thoughts and outrage with the world.

The Vick story was naturally of great interest to the Humane Society. Carie Lewis, the organization's director of emerging media, was already tracking what people were saying about the scandal on channels such as MySpace, Facebook, and blogs. Carie was not new to these spaces; she and her colleagues had launched and reiterated a series of experiments on multiple social media channels such as MySpace where they already had 17,000 friends.

But then Carie found something unexpected on YouTube. Animal lovers were posting their own videos denouncing Michael Vick and dogfighting. Carie decided the Humane Society needed to follow their lead.

Figure 9.1
The Winning Humane Society Video: *Ms. Paisley Sky*

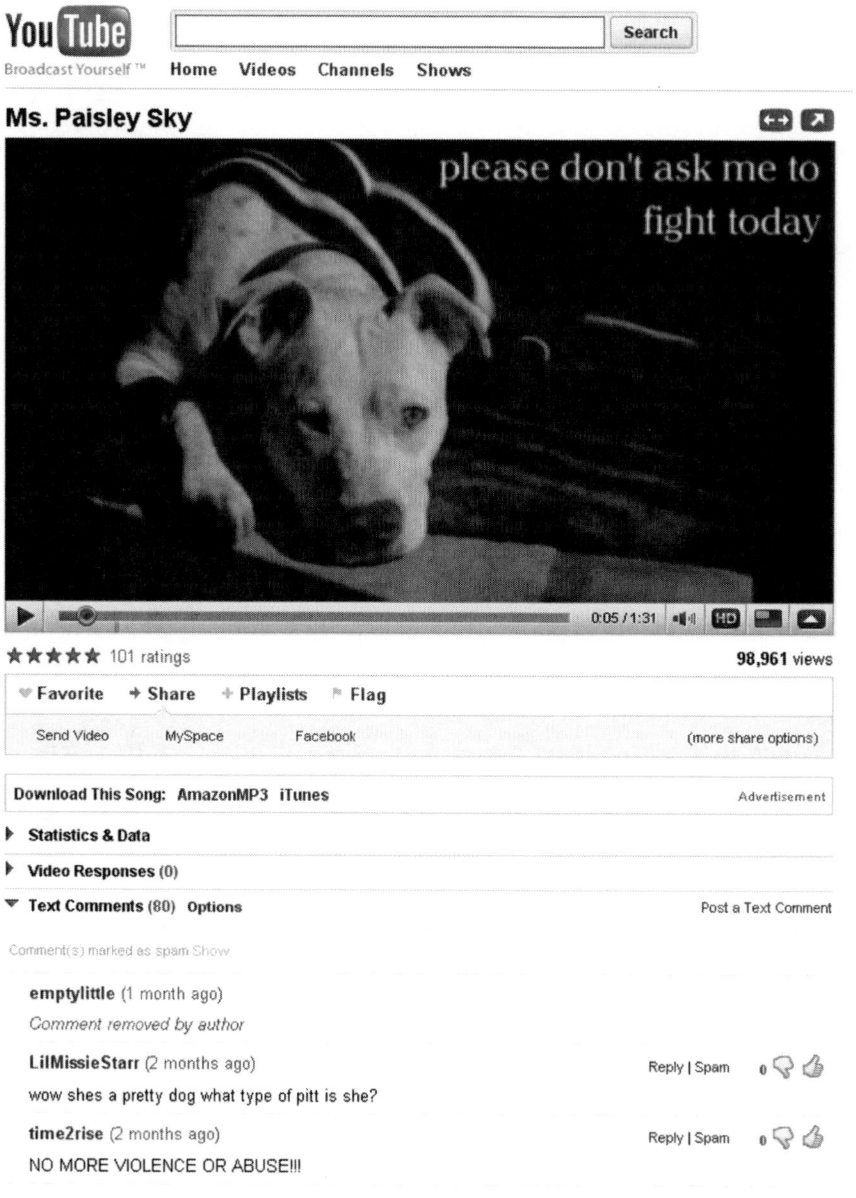

Source: Reprinted with the permission of The Humane Society of the United States.

As a result, the Humane Society launched the "Knock Out Animal Fighting YouTube Contest" just a few weeks after the Vick story broke. Anyone who was outraged by the story was invited to post their own video about how they felt about dogfighting. They could then upload these videos to the Humane Society's Web site and the Humane Society's YouTube channel. The public could view and vote on the videos.

The audience viewed the resulting twenty-two video submissions hundreds of thousands of times. The winning video (Figure 9.1) was viewed over 115,000 times alone. This demonstrates the 1:10:100 rule of user-generated content—that for every one person who creates content, ten share it and one hundred view it.[1]

Ultimately, the crowd chose one winner, and the organization chose another and turned it into a public service announcement. The contest was more than group catharsis, however. Carie and her colleagues encouraged every viewer, every blogger, and every Humane Society member to talk to their friends about turning their energy and anger into positive action. They wanted dog lovers to advocate for anti-dogfighting legislation at the state level. This kind of advocacy was the ultimate measure of success for their efforts.

Carie used a process we call **learning loops** to monitor and analyze the video contest as it unfolded (see Figure 9.2). She analyzed which topics gained more

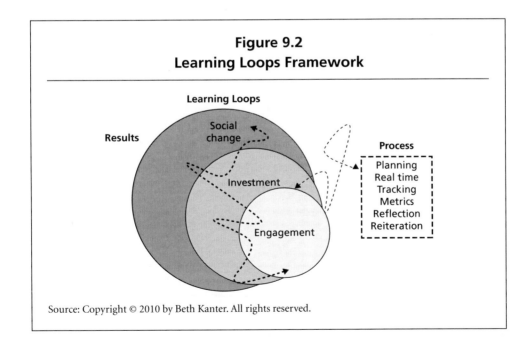

**Figure 9.2
Learning Loops Framework**

traction for discussions, which parts of her network responded to particular messages or activities, and which influencers could be engaged for the contest and beyond. She also did content analysis of the comments on YouTube and recognized the patterns of people's feelings about the contest, dogfighting, and the Humane Society.

However, learning loops is more than tracking and monitoring results in real time. It also incorporates a process of reflection at the end of a project. Carie explains, "Our end-of-project debrief answers one question: Was it worth it? That helps us to learn how to improve our strategy for the next experiment or project."[2]

According to Carie, the video contest was worth doing because the Humane Society learned that

- It needed ways for supporters to participate in video contests in addition to producing videos. These included voting and commenting.

- The number of video submissions is only one measure for engaging people through video contests. Additional measures include the number of people discussing the contest online, page views, and other awareness metrics.

- Using the organization's e-mail list, which grew by three thousand names as a result of the contest, engaged more people as voters and commentators on the videos.

- Monitoring a time-sensitive contest or event by listening using relevant keywords and analyzing comments and links as they happen is crucial for making real-time adjustments.

- Going where the video content was developing, meaning YouTube, made their campaign more findable. It also increased their search results on Google.

- The free, original content created for the contest could continue to live online and on broadcast media through the public service announcement.

- Posting the winners on the Humane Society Web site increased traffic there.

- The contest helped the organization build its relationships with influential bloggers. The organization has continued to develop these relationships over time for future efforts.

The success of the Michael Vick video contest was possible because the Humane Society had been using learning loops from project to project over the course of several years. This success was then paid forward to inform and guide the next iteration of projects and experiments.

Before beginning a more thorough discussion of learning loops, it is important to clarify two possible misinterpretations of them. First, we are not suggesting that organizations change their strategies minute to minute based on what they just heard or learned. Organizations need to be intentional about their efforts and allow them to unfold over time. That said, real-time improvements can be made to an effort without affecting long-term intentions. The Humane Society did this when it added a public service announcement component to their video contest as it was running.

Second, we'd like to dispel the assumption that fast and flexible learning happens in a vacuum. Learning loops are tied to an organization's on-land implementation and measurement efforts. Learning loops focus on measuring an organization's use of social media. They do not substitute for other assessments and evaluations; rather, they are another technique in the organizational learning toolbox.

In this chapter, we will dissect the different parts of learning loops that include planning, real-time monitoring, and measuring engagement. We will also outline the reflection process that organizations with successful learning loops use on a regular basis, as well as steps for understanding the financial return for organizations from their social media investments as well as the social impact.

PLANNING LEARNING LOOPS

It is imperative for organizations to carefully consider their goals and learning objectives for using social media prior to starting a project. Alexandra Samuel, a nonprofit social media consultant, cautions about a common pitfall: "The greatest peril of social media is analytophilia. It's about obsessing on raw numbers and constantly checking your stats without a clear idea of what you're looking for."[3] Indeed, data are relatively easy to collect online, increasing the risk of gathering enormous amounts of useless data.

So organizations must first think through what they want to learn. They can begin by

• **Picking a specific, narrow objective**. One challenge in using social media strategically is to resist the inclination to try to reach the whole wide world on the World Wide Web. Identify a specific target audience for any effort. We have discussed many instances where something goes viral, and many people are attracted to a cause and moved to share information or click in support of an organization. But these efforts began as conversations with a small, select group of people. Organizations need to zero in on who cares about this particular effort most. Who has the skills or expertise we need the most? Who has the greatest influence in this network?

• **Designing low-cost, low-risk experiments**. Using social media lends itself to small, inexpensive experiments as discussed in the previous chapter about microplanning. The experiment can be as simple as allocating thirty minutes a day for a staff person to use Twitter to connect with journalists and influential Twitter users. Or it could be facilitating a conversation on Facebook to crowdsource a new fundraising effort.

• **Articulating key learning questions**. Organizations should articulate a few questions that they want to learn about their use of social media as their experiment unfolds. Focus these questions on the effort's immediate results, who is doing what using social media, and then find relevant metrics to track. For example, if the experiment focuses on Twitter outreach, questions could include whether the number of followers is increasing and what issues and topics this community finds particularly interesting. The metrics could include the number of followers gained, the number of messages forwarded on Twitter (or "retweeted" in Twitter lingo), or the number of clicks on a link to the organization's blog or Web site. Free tools to aid in this analysis include, but are not limited to, Twitalyzer, Bit.ly, and TweetEffect.

Having considered these issues, an organization is now ready to begin measuring how social media is working for a particular effort.

MEASURING ENGAGEMENT AND CONNECTIONS

As we have discussed throughout this book, connecting with people is the first step in a process of engaging and building relationships with them. The later stages ultimately produce actions for social change.

In the analog world, it was difficult to trace how people created and sustained relationships. In the digital world, however, organizations can follow the bouncing ball of conversations and actions across the Web and better understand how to stimulate, broaden, and deepen conversations about causes and organizations.

One particularly important vehicle for strengthening connections between people and organizations are blogs. An organization with a blog has multiple options for measuring whether and how it is deepening its engagement and relationship with its readers. These include

- **Number of subscribers**. There are two different kinds of blog readers: subscribers and visitors. Subscribers have made a commitment to regularly receive (and hopefully read or at least scan) a blog. Visitors are people who occasionally visit the blog. Increasing the number of subscribers is critical to growing an audience of people who care about a blog. It is also important to find out why readers unsubscribe from the blog. If the organization has the unsubscriber's e-mail address, it should send a follow-up e-mail and a minisurvey asking why the person chose to unsubscribe. The organization may learn that the blog's topics, schedule, or even tone of voice were key factors in the unsubscribe decision.

- **Monthly trends**. Reviewing monthly trends of which posts are read and commented on will help the blog writers understand how to better connect with and engage the readers. Monthly trends include the number of readers, of course, but also keyword analysis of which topics were of particular interest to readers and other bloggers.

- **Engagement metrics**. Many free, online tools exist for measuring the type and depth of engagement. One Web site, PostRank, ranks the engagement of blog posts with a number from one to ten. It bases the scores on the "five C's" of engagement: creating, critiquing, chatting, collecting, and clicking. Organizations should examine what topics and styles drive the highest-scoring posts. Are these posts longer and more in-depth, or shorter and focused on one topic? Do they include information from a lot of outside resources? Is the tone formal or informal? Do they include tips? What is the quality of the conversation in the comments section? What did you learn from the conversation your readers started? If you have a group blog, are there differences between authors? Why? Did anything surprise you? In addition, comparing the highest- and lowest-ranked posts may prove illuminating and help improve the blog's quality.

- **Bookmarking**. Using a tool like Delicious, bloggers can find out whether readers are bookmarking that blog's pages for future reading. This is important to track because blog content bookmarked on social networking sites tends to attract additional readers. Again, the blogger should evaluate the topics and styles of her most-bookmarked posts to see what works.

- **Comments**. Comments are the most obvious and powerful measure of reader engagement. The common ratio is that a blog will have one commentator for every one hundred readers. People who post comments are highly motivated individuals who tend to strongly agree or disagree with the post. Each comment is one part of a larger conversation happening on that blog. The blogger should help facilitate the conversation by joining in the comments.

  Using Joost Blog Metrics on Wordpress illustrates the post-to-comment ratio. Review the comments and their content on a monthly basis to see what kind of relationship your blog has with its readers. Which topics encourage the most comments? Do posts with more questions in the title and questions in the end generate more comments? Did you do any outreach on other channels like Twitter to encourage commenting? Is a conversation happening among people who comment? What do you do to facilitate it? What's the quality of the commenting? Are you learning? When and why are the comments positive or negative?

- **Influence**. Blogs are not stand-alone entities. Each one is part of a much larger conversation within the blogosphere, the community of blogs. Influential blogs catalyze conversations on other blogs. A measure of influence is called *authority*, meaning the number of blogs linking to one blog. Increasing a blog's authority increases its influence in the blogosphere. Tools such as Technorati and Yahoo! Site Explorer can measure blog authority.

  Bloggers should also track the number of incoming links to their blogs through their blogs' analytics packages. Linking is the commerce of the blogosphere, and it is expected to be reciprocal. Bloggers who are generous in their linking to other blogs will see the same in return. And as we know from Chapter Three, "Understanding Social Networks," these reciprocal relationships transform themselves into social capital.

- **Industry index**. There are a growing number of sites and lists of influential nonprofit blogs and bloggers. For example, the List of Change catalogues several hundred nonprofit blogs according to a host of metrics about their influence. Nonprofit bloggers should regularly review the lists to understand their influence better and connect with them.

Digging deeper into blog reader engagement might seem like a lot of work, but with practice and discipline, it can take only an hour or two a month to gather data about an organization's efforts on its blogs and on other social media channels like Facebook or Twitter. The next important step is using the data as part of a regular process of organizational reflection.

REFLECTIONS

Organizations need to carve out time to take a deep breath and reflect on what has gone well, what hasn't, and how they can move forward. Learning, adapting, and preparing for the next iterative effort is the secret to getting tangible results from your social media efforts.

Reflection only works, however, when organizations value learning over blaming and treat the process as a search for insight. Let's imagine that an organization launched a video contest and four people submitted entries. Organizations ready to cast blame might castigate the organizing team and vow never to engage in such silliness again. But a team focused on reflection and adaptation could start a conversation internally and discuss improvements for the next contest or crowdsourcing effort.

Wendy Harman, social media manager for the Red Cross, described her organization's approach to reflection this way: "At first, I would do the reflection myself, using a journal to document the experiment, and at the end of the project review everything [I had] collected. I'd think about successes and failures. I also kept an eye on what other nonprofits were doing in the social media space. This would inevitably lead to the design of the next experiment. Now that our organization has embraced social media, we do this as a team."[4]

Organizations also need to step back from the daily whirlwind of metrics and take one to two hours a month to wrestle with the larger questions of how social media fits into their overall efforts. They need to ask: Which vehicles and channels help us gain the most traction? How should we adjust our workload internally to reflect those results? How are our social media activities helping us meet our overall strategic goals? How are our efforts using social media supporting our on-land activities?

Reflection does not have to be a private activity. It can be done in connected, transparent ways. The organization's blog can be a place to share lessons learned with readers and to ask them for their feedback and suggestions as well. The result: a powerful way to learn and improve over time.

RETURN ON INVESTMENT

Networked Nonprofits understand the value of measuring connections and engagements using social media. But they also know they need to demonstrate value in order to sustain and extend their work. By taking the approaches we've outlined in this chapter, it is not a difficult leap to translate results into a financial return for an organization.

Analyzing return on investment includes the benefits, costs, and value of an effort using social media over time. Benefits may be intangible (cannot be translated into a dollar amount and are usually behavior oriented) or tangible (those that can be translated into dollar or time savings). One way to understand the financial return of an effort is by using comparable costs from more traditional, analog approaches.

Table 9.1 presents a comparison of activities using social media with traditional approaches and their associated costs.

Table 9.1
Knock Out Animal Fighting YouTube Contest

Social Media Approach	Traditional Approach
Listening online	Purchasing formal market research
Cultivating relationships with bloggers and reporters online that result in posts and stories	Hiring communications staff or a press agent to place stories in the mainstream media
Using free online services like Facebook or Twitter to announce an event	Placing an ad in a newspaper
Generating content that can be turned into a public service announcement	Producing your own PSA video content
Asking supporters to share news and information with their friends on social networking sites	Disseminating information to the public through newsletters and press releases
Using the organization's blog, YouTube, Facebook, or Twitter presence to drive Web site traffic	Buying Google ads and hiring a search engine optimization consultant
Acquiring e-mail addresses from people who share them via Twitter, blogs, or social networking profiles	Purchasing e-mail addresses

An organization can also craft a new experiment in which the costs and return on investment are very clearly embedded within the experiment from the beginning.

SOCIAL CHANGE

Affecting social change is, of course, the ultimate goal for nonprofit organizations. Connecting with people and deepening engagement are important building blocks for creating friends, readers, and followers, but social change happens when these people do something on the organization's behalf such as donating food to a food bank, distributing coats in winter, passing legislation, and funding cancer research. As we have mentioned throughout this book, social media plays an important part in the total social change equation, but it is only a part of a larger endeavor. Social media can be used to affect change directly.

A great example of social media being used to affect change were the immigration marches of 2006. That spring, tens of thousands of young people around the country organized themselves to march for immigration reform. In Los Angeles alone, over sixty thousand young people hit the streets to march. Social media tools, such as text messaging and particularly MySpace, were integral to the organizing efforts. But the organizing didn't stop when the marchers showed up. The organizers and participants continued to use a variety of tools to coordinate meeting places and messages as marches unfolded.

CONCLUSION

It's always been important for organizations to develop a variety of measures to create a rich picture of how, why, and whether their efforts are succeeding. We now need to use learning loops and add social media measurement to the mix.

Learning loops unwind over the course of multiple efforts (see Table 9.2). Monitoring helps organizations adjust sagging efforts immediately. Stronger programs and processes increase online supporters' engagement. Organizations can see a significant financial return from a well-executed campaign. And when it's all done well, nonprofits will see the ultimate measure of social media's value.

Table 9.2
Learning Loops Framework

Framework	Result
Engagement	Interaction
	Reputation
	Influence
	Loyalty
	Satisfaction
	Sentiment
	Feedback
	Share message with friends
Return on Investment	Web-site traffic
	Web-site conversions to e-mail list
	Sign-ups
	Donations
	Leads
	Blog subscribers
	Members
	Signed online petitions
	Calls or e-mails to government officials
Social Change	Saved the whales
	Switched to compact lightbulbs
	Prevented malaria
	Reduced teen pregnancy
	Achieved peace on Earth
	Lowered the Earth's temperature 5 degrees

REFLECTION QUESTIONS

Measurement

- Are you developing the tools and methods to measure success (that is, going beyond clicks and impressions)?

- Are you synthesizing qualitative insights in addition to analyzing hard data points?

Learning

- Are you tweaking your strategy along the way—and adapting where change may be needed?
- Can staff create low-risk pilot projects prior to scrutinizing them through traditional ROI exercises?
- Do you implement initiatives that will help your organization learn prior to investing in major marketing campaigns?

Adapting

- Are you making time for reflection at the end of the project?
- Are you revising the design of a project based on what you've learned?

ROI

- What are the benefits from the project?
- How can you translate these benefits into dollar amounts or time saved?

You can also use this set of questions for reflection at the end:

- What worked really well in this social media project?
- Did it accomplish our goals or outcomes? In what ways?
- Did it fall short? Why?
- What would you do differently?
- What surprises came up during the project? What could you learn or capture from them?
- What insights did you gain during the project?
- What processes did you use that worked well? What didn't work so well? Why?
- How did people work together? Were there conflicts? How were they handled? Did people gain any new insights or perspectives as a result?
- Were there people or perspectives missing from this project that you would include the next time?

- What skills and processes did you help people learn as part of this project? What skills and processes would you spend time on if you did this over again?

- What were the most innovative aspects of the project? How did they work?

- What did you do in this project that you could transfer to other projects?

- What is the most troubling aspect of the project? What might you do to deal with it differently?

- What skills came in most handy during this project? What skills did this project make you realize you need to acquire?

- What really puzzles you about this project? What are the unanswered questions you have about what happened?

- What intrigues you about this project?

- What would you like to learn more about that would help this (or other projects) in the future?

- Where did we mess up? Make mistakes? Fall on our face? What can we learn from this?

chapter TEN

From Friending to Funding

O n September 7, 2006, Scott Harrison turned thirty-one years old. He decided to celebrate by inviting his friends to attend a party. But in lieu of gifts, he asked them each to donate $20 to charity: water, a nonprofit he had recently started to fund clean drinking water in developing countries. Seven hundred people attended the party and raised enough money to underwrite six drinking wells in Uganda.

Scott has many great talents. One in particular is his ability to make friends wherever he goes. He makes them in New York where he lives, on Facebook and Twitter, and on a rural road in Liberia. He is also a great storyteller and passionate advocate for his cause. He has infused his organization with this socialness. At the time of this writing, charity: water had over 44,000 friends on Facebook and over a million followers on Twitter. These friends tell other people about the work that charity: water does. Searching for charity: water on Google brings up over 20 million results.

Scott and his staff have also succeeded in turning these friends into funders for their organization (see Figure 10.1). Three years after the organization began, charity: water had raised over $10 million to fund 1,341 clean water projects that serve 727,110 people.[1]

Charity: water demonstrates the effectiveness of working as a Networked Nonprofit. It does so by

- **Being transparent**. The organization operates out in the open. Annual reports, financial statements, and audit reports are posted online. How projects are evaluated and how the money is used is available on the organization's Web site. People can easily reach the staff on a variety of social media channels including their Web site, Facebook, and Twitter.

Figure 10.1
*my*charity: water Is charity: water's Social Network of Donors

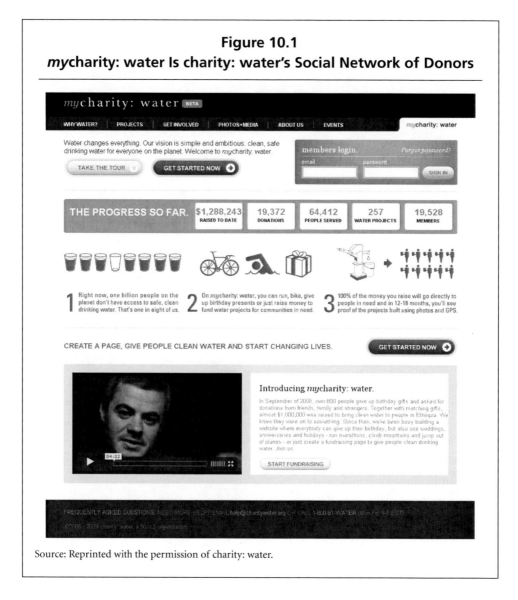

Source: Reprinted with the permission of charity: water.

In addition, every donation is tied to a specific clean water project. Donors can view pictures of the clean water project that they helped to fund online and through Google Earth.

- **Being simple.** charity: water has a simple message that is easy to communicate online, particularly on Twitter with its 140-character limit: *charity: water creates clean water in developing countries.* That's it. charity: water sticks to what it does best, raising awareness and funds for clean water. It networks the rest by partnering with organizations with long track records of implementing clean water systems in Rwanda, Uganda, Malawi, Kenya, Central African Republic, Ethiopia, Bangladesh, India, and Honduras.

- **Listening, engaging, and building relationships.** Wherever the organization is online and on land, its goal is to engage many people in conversations about the horrific fact that over a billion people live with dirty and disease-ridden drinking water. charity: water is constantly listening online and sharing and connecting with people on multiple channels.

Being a Networked Nonprofit has enabled charity: water to raise money from their large network of friends. In 2009, charity: water created a special area of its Web site called *my*charity: water, where individuals create their own fundraising efforts on behalf of the organization. Thousands of people joined in by forgoing birthday presents in lieu of donations, and walking, swimming, and running to raise over half a million dollars for the year.

During Twestival, the worldwide fundraising event organized by Amanda Rose and her friends, charity: water followed and led in equal measure. They let people do things on their behalf without worrying about losing control.

The organization's accomplishments haven't all happened online. In-person parties and gatherings, news media articles, and marketing and advertising campaigns have raised awareness and money for the organization as well. charity: water is marrying traditional forms of fundraising with social media to turn friends into funders and, along with other organizations, providing a new blueprint for fundraising for the future.

In this chapter, we will discuss the current state of fundraising, the elements necessary to turn friends into funders, examples of organizations doing just that, and their lessons learned.

WHERE FUNDING STANDS TODAY

In his book *CauseWired*, Tom Watson pointed out this astounding fact: "Even in the most charitable country on Earth [the United States], giving remains stagnant as a factor of our national wealth."[2] Indeed, though the number of nonprofit organizations has exploded, and the number of requests for donations and ways to give has expanded, the total amount of giving as a percentage of the wealth of the country has not increased at all. No definitive reason explains why this is the case. But one contributing factor is that organizations have settled into their tried-and-true methods for raising funds—such as special events, large individual donations, and mailings to their donor bases—while failing to increase the pool of people being captured through these activities.

Some of these activities like Twestival appeal to young people, but many, particularly direct mail fundraising, do not. Organizations need to set their sights on the future and reach out to young people as donors. Even if this age group doesn't have large amounts to give yet, developing their giving practices early leads to more giving over the course of a lifetime. It is incumbent on nonprofit organizations to connect with this new generation where they are most active and comfortable, which is online.

We understand that it is difficult to break old habits when the pressure is mounting to make payroll and pay the bills. Consider the circumstances: A deep recession, huge competition among organizations for funds, a stagnant pool of traditional donors, and donor fatigue with transactional interactions all add up to trouble on the fundraising front for many nonprofit organizations. However, organizations need to begin to experiment with new fundraising models to supplement the old ones to ensure that they are sustainable in the future.

Clearly, organizations must raise money from a variety of different sources, and that mix now includes social media. However, fundraising online or using social media is *not* a panacea to these problems. For all the promise and excitement of online fundraising, it represents only a small sliver of the total donations made to nonprofit organizations to date. To put online fundraising into perspective, a survey conducted by the software company Blackbaud in 2009 found that 7 percent of the total donations for seventy-five of the largest nonprofits in the country came in online.[3]

But online fundraising is growing quickly. The percentage in the Blackbaud survey was half that just two years prior. One week after the enormous earthquake struck Haiti in early 2010, the American Red Cross reported raising $22 million by text message. A study shortly thereafter reported that 37 percent of donors reported giving for Haitian relief online or by text message.[4]

It is incumbent upon organizations to energetically begin to figure out how to turn their online friends into funders.

Successful fundraising happens through relationship building, and using social media to raise funds is no exception to that rule. As Betsy Harman, a fundraising consultant in Chicago, says, "Any nonprofit who thinks they can simply put a 'donate now' button on their Web site, or slap up [a] Causes page on Facebook and wait for the money to roll in, doesn't understand online fundraising. It's still all about building relationships, telling your story, and taking potential donors through the process of cultivation, stewardship, and solicitation."[5]

Let's break down electronic giving into two component parts. Giving electronically through portals, such as a "Donate Here" button on a Web site, is one form of giving. This differs from giving on social media channels like Facebook, where friends are turned into donors for a cause or nonprofit organization. Turning friends into funders on social media channels is at an even earlier stage of development than general online giving. For instance, a survey of nonprofit organizations released in April 2009 by the Nonprofit Technology Network (NTEN) and the consulting firm Common Knowledge found that only 39.9 percent of respondents had raised money on Facebook, and another 29.1 percent had raised less than $500 over the past twelve months.[6]

Amounts raised online will grow as people become more comfortable giving online and as more organizations become fluent using online fundraising tools. However, as with all good fundraising, building the relationships that are key to long-term giving takes time. Building an online community of supporters who want to donate can take six to eighteen months. Organizations that have successfully raised money using social media have focused on iterative experiments. This inexpensive approach helps them learn and improve over time. As social media consultant Ivan Booth observed, "It's about cultivating relationships with your most passionate supporters, giving them ways to speak in their own voice, and connecting them with other people. This doesn't happen overnight."[7]

Organizations also need to begin to connect with young people as donors in ways that are comfortable and meaningful to them.

Joe Green is the cofounder of Causes for Facebook, an application that enables Facebook users to make their friends aware of a cause and fundraise for it. Green explains the power of online social networks as donation vehicles for young people: "With techniques like direct mail for fundraising, the organization is seeking out the donor, knocking on their door. With social networks, it is much more a marketplace dynamic because these younger potential donors are seeking out issues on places like Facebook and then they serendipitously discover the organizations. A lot of younger people are new donors and haven't been engaged before. This is their point of entry. For better or worse, brand equity is less important on social networks."[8]

Indeed, Facebook is one channel that organizations use to engage their network in conversation about an issue, raise awareness, build relationships, organize events, and over time, raise money. Wick Davis, director of online services for the Lupus Foundation of America (LFA), said about his organization's use of Facebook: "I really see LFA's Facebook cause [as] an important outpost on social networks. As a result of our constant engagement with our members, we've increased our Cause membership 584 percent in six months. And we've increased our online donations in Facebook by 790 percent in the same time frame."[9]

While younger donors are critical to long-term giving, breaking through to new donors of any age is still imperative for organizations' future sustainability. For example, organizations who successfully raised funds online for America's Giving Challenge (the Case Foundation–sponsored contest that Peggy Padden did so well in) found that on average 60 percent of the new Facebook friends and donors they made through the Challenge were new to their organizations.[10]

SOCIAL MEDIA FUNDRAISING PATTERNS

A small number of nonprofit organizations that adopted social media and social networking sites early are now beginning to raise large amounts of money online. These include charity: water, Epic Change, The Nature Conservancy, The Humane Society of the United States, and the American Red Cross. In addition to the characteristics of Networked Nonprofits discussed previously in this book, these organizations have discovered that turning online friends into funders requires a few additional components:

• **Social media are part of a multichannel strategy**. Using social media channels alone for fundraising will not be as effective as making them a part of a multichannel strategy that includes traditional fundraising techniques. This includes using e-mail, Web site presence, Google ads, face-to-face events, and reaching out to the mainstream media.

A great example of how well this multichannel approach works is the Humane Society's Spay Day, an annual campaign on the last Tuesday of February that inspires people to save animal lives by spaying or neutering pets and feral cats. For years the organization had been building friendships on social networking sites but not asking them for funds. In 2009, the organization launched the United States Spay Day Photo Contest as one part of its overall effort, in addition to traditional broadcast media and other social media outreach.

The contest took place on Facebook, where more than 45,000 pet lovers entered their pets' photos and encouraged their friends to raise money for spay/ neuter efforts worldwide. It raised more than $550,000, with the top five hundred fundraisers receiving $25 gift certificates. The crowd and a panel of celebrity judges selected the winning photos, which received $1,000 each.

Grace Markarian, online communications manager at the Humane Society, said that integrating social media into their fundraising campaign ". . . helped us increase awareness and reach audiences that we would not have normally reached."[11]

• **People are partners, not ATM machines**. Reflecting on the future of online fundraising, Peter Dietz, founder of Social Actions, wrote, "Individuals will come to your organization with the expectation of being full partners in your work, not just dollar wells to be tapped when cash is needed. Donations will be a consequence of meaningful engagement, not a measurement of it."[12]

A compelling example is WildlifeDirect, a nonprofit based in Nairobi, Kenya. According to Paula Kahumbu, executive director, "In 2004, a group of committed conservationists, led by Dr. Richard Leakey, became convinced that social networks provided the best opportunity for securing a future for wildlife—an approach that could harness the collective energy of countless good conservationists and combine it with millions of individuals around the world who have a genuine concern for the future of the planet's wildlife and unique habitats."

In 2007, WildlifeDirect had seven blogs, each written about a specific animal by a conservation professional in the Democratic Republic of Congo. The blogs were an opportunity to engage people in conversations about the daily challenge of conservation work in Africa. They also raised $350,000 to pay rangers' salaries and help save mountain gorillas in the Virunga National Park. Says Paula, "Two years later, we have over seventy blogs, [and] donations have risen fourfold, as has Web site visitation. We treat our donors as partners in our programs."

The WildlifeDirect blogs enable individual donors around the world to communicate directly with the people that they are funding. This crowd can respond to any conservation emergency much more swiftly and efficiently than large bureaucratic agencies, and help reverse the catastrophic loss of habitats and species and secure the future of wildlife in Africa, Asia, and around the world.[13]

• **Storytelling makes fundraising personal**. Storytelling brings alive the activities of an organization and makes their issues real and urgent for current and potential supporters. Stories put a human face on abstract ideas, provide moral clarity in a fight against unfairness, right a fundamental wrong, and celebrate triumphs over evil. Thomas Jefferson may have been the most brilliant philosopher and writer of the Revolutionary War period, but Ben Franklin was the best storyteller, and his printing press churned out the stories (some real, some fictional) that moved people to action.

Stories are also dramatic and empowering and strengthen connections between people. We know by heart the personal stories that catalyzed causes and nonprofit organizations: a young boy, Ryan White, and his heroic battle to live with AIDS; Lois Gibbs discovering that her entire neighborhood of Love Canal, New York, was built on a toxic waste dump that was poisoning her three children and seven hundred of their neighbors; the chilling story and sweet face of a missing boy, Adam Walsh, that started a national movement to track and find missing children. These tragic stories moved large numbers of people and institutions to action.

Organizations can use social media such as blogs and YouTube to broadcast these stories to the world instantly, easily, and inexpensively. Cecile Richards, the president of the Planned Parenthood Federation of America, said, "There are millions of stories inside of Planned Parenthood. Women have started to write on Facebook and blog amazing stories about the first time they went to Planned Parenthood. We have to tell their stories, to put a human face on the work we're doing."[14]

Let's look at some other examples of storytelling in action. Sanjay Patel and Stacey Monk founded a nonprofit organization, Epic Change, in 2008. The organization piloted an effort that first year by providing loans to support the Shephard Junior primary school in Arusha, Tanzania. Its effort seemed similar in design to Kiva and other microenterprise loan efforts. But then the organization took an interesting turn with this sentence on its Web site: "'How can loans be repaid by sharing stories?' we asked." Stacey listed an impressive array of ways, including

- Organizing local performances and auctions
- Selling products like cards and candles with the photos, stories, and artwork of students
- Writing grants that share the story of the school's charismatic founder, Mama Lucy Kamptoni
- Creating and selling a book

As of summer 2009, $5,000 of the original $65,000 loan had been repaid through these activities.[15]

Storytelling using social media provides opportunities for individuals to use a megaphone they would not have had access to before. Change.org, a vibrant online platform for in-depth discussions about issues like animal rights, global warming, and human trafficking, learned about the power of personal storytelling on their area dedicated to homelessness.

Shannon Moriarity, Change.org's facilitator for the homelessness area, wrote a post on December 10, 2008, entitled "Choosing Streets Over Shelters." It spoke about why a homeless person would choose to live in the streets rather than stay in a shelter. A number of professionals in the field of homelessness wrote comments about the post on the site. And then came SlumJack Homeless. He was currently homeless and shared his personal story of why he would rather live on the streets than in a shelter.

"Shelters," he wrote, "are often euphemized as 'emergency shelter' . . . but the emergency is that you have nowhere else to just be and operate, so being AT a 'shelter' is the emergency. And being in that predicament, even with the 'help' of merely having a lousy place to sleep indoors, a disgusting bathroom, and a gesture of a 'meal'—*at best*—just perpetuates your true problem."[16]

Ben Rattray, the founder and CEO of Change.org, reflected about why SlumJack Homeless's voice is so important: "Among the many limitations of traditional media is the limitation on who gets to speak. The Internet democratizes that access. It empowers even the most marginalized people to be heard—the homeless veteran, the undocumented immigrant, the prostitute. This is important not just for those who are usually objects of discussion to speak on their own behalf, but for those who can now hear them—unadulterated, personal, and authentic. It's the personal connection that this rare first person narrative forges with the reader that creates real empathy and changed perspectives."[17]

Organizations can help individuals tell their stories on behalf of the organization in a variety of ways:

- Offer fact sheets and other information that individuals can roll into their own storytelling as Change.org does on their blogs.

- Provide platforms for individuals to tell their own stories without editing or filtering them. Global Reach is an Internet radio station that provides opportunities for people around the globe to share their personal stories.

- Encourage individuals to act as their own creative directors and "mash up" different media to tell a story. Valdis Krebs and Cleveland City Council member Anthony Brancatelli used a variety of public data about foreclosures in the Slavic Village neighborhood of Cleveland. They mapped the patterns to the mortgage lending practices that led to the foreclosures and found that most of them could be traced to a single, nefarious, family-owned subprime mortgage company trying to cover its tracks.[18]

- **Thankfulness makes donors want to give more**. Thanking supporters has too often become a mechanical reflex for organizations, limited to providing documentation for tax purposes to donors. Sincere thanking of supporters needs to happen often and enthusiastically for people to feel truly connected to organizations. And it doesn't even have to happen for a particular reason.

One congregation we know asked their board members to call twenty congregants over a two-week period to thank them for being members. That was it—they simply thanked them for being members of their community. They didn't have any ulterior motive, and it wasn't a setup for fundraising. It took about two or three hours of time for each board member to make all of their calls. Once congregants overcame their initial surprise and suspicion, they were delighted to talk with board members.

Congregants' reactions to the calls ranged from happy to ecstatic. They had a few pent-up complaints about the institution, but about half of the congregants also offered to volunteer in the office and at holiday time. And it cost nothing except for a few hours of volunteer time.

In comparison, fundraising calls for this congregation typically had a 10 to 20 percent positive response with low dollar amounts pledged, and the other 80 to 90 percent of the congregants running for the hills hoping not to be asked to give.

Thanking needs to be quick, sincere, and as personal as possible. People have many options for causes to support, and people who feel underappreciated will find other homes for their passions. Social media makes thanking people easier and more public than ever. And the ways to thank donors and volunteers using social media are only limited by the thanker's imagination.

For example, organizations can list the names of donors (who want to be named) on their blogs and Web sites. They can send a personal e-mail to donors. They can use Facebook and Twitter not only to thank people personally, but also to let their entire community of friends and followers see the thanks. Of course, none of these methods precludes organizations from also picking up the phone or sending donors a personal thank-you letter via snail mail.

Organizations are beginning to experiment with a variety of ways of using social media for fundraising. Two particular models of raising friends for funds that have gained traction recently are clicking for causes and contests.

- **Clicking to leverage donation dollars.** Some organizations successfully raise money on social networks such as Facebook or Twitter when the donors click to support a cause or raise friends for a cause, and by doing so, leverage a donation from a sponsor.

But in fact, nonprofits have used click actions on their Web sites long before Facebook and Twitter existed.[19] For instance, the FreeRice game, an interactive online game that donates grains of rice to the United Nations World Food Program, launched in 2007. Users click to play a word game, which in turn leverages a donation to fight hunger around the world. For each click, private sponsors such as Citibank, Unilever, and Credit Suisse donate ten grains of rice. This may not seem like a lot, but when millions of people are clicking, it adds up to a lot of food very quickly. The result: As of October 2009, FreeRice has donated a total of 70,991,387,110 grains of rice.[20]

Another example of "click for dollars" comes from one of the most popular and engaging applications on Facebook—(Lil) Green Patch. This social gardening application lets Facebook users plant a virtual garden on their profile and send virtual plants as gifts to their friends. Advertisers donate money to causes when people give gifts. The Nature Conservancy has raised over $125,000 from advertising clicks this way. The application is particularly engaging for younger people and educates them about the plight of the rain forest, thus combining self-expression and virtual gift giving.

TwitCause is a Twitter application similar to the popular fundraising **application causes** on Facebook. As a basic service, TwitCause identifies a cause to support (partially based on community feedback) and uses Twitter to drive awareness for it and donations. TwitCause has also identified sponsors willing to make a donation for each follower raised on Twitter. Ice cream maker Häagen-Dazs stepped up to save endangered honeybees. They donated $1 for the first five hundred people to send a Twitter message with the code #HelpHoneyBees. The money supported a UC Davis research project on the devastation of honeybee colonies, as well as the Häagen-Dazs Honey Bee Haven, which teaches people about creating their own honeybee farms. The campaign generated over 290,000 tweets about the campaign.[21]

• **Conducting online fundraising contests**. A growing number of online fundraising contests have enabled groups to raise significant funds. America's Giving Challenge, sponsored by The Case Foundation, started the trend in late 2007. In total, the first Giving Challenge enabled over six thousand causes to raise about $1.8 million.[22]

And in 2009, Target Corporation launched Bullseye Gives on Facebook. The giving effort asked Facebook users to vote on how Target should allocate $3 million among ten large nonprofit organizations such as the American Red Cross and St. Jude's Children's Research Hospital.

Taken together, all these experiments create a picture of best practices to inform future friends-to-funding efforts.

SUCCESSFUL ONLINE FUNDRAISING TACTICS WITH SOCIAL MEDIA

The common characteristics of successful fundraising efforts using social media include the following:

• **Credibility**. Organizations can't just appear and ask for money. They have to establish trust with potential donors first to make fundraising appeals credible and meaningful to people. As stated above, organizations need to invest in relationship building before launching campaigns.

• **Simple, compelling messages**. We have gone from using the analogy of a thirty-second elevator speech for fundraising to a 140-character message on Twitter as the model for a fundraising pitch. Fundraising messages using social media must be short and easily understood. Of course, communicating an organization's entire purpose may not be possible in such a small space, but it's good practice to reduce a fundraising pitch to its essence this way. Successful fundraising pitches for social media boil down to this formula: "Your Donation Will Help Us Get to This Result."

- **Urgency**. Building urgency around fundraising is especially critical for online outreach, where attention spans are shorter than ever. Intensive fundraising efforts should have clear, short deadlines. It is better to set a short time with low expectations than to make the effort too long and the goal too high. Urgency also comes from knowing how well an organization is doing in real time. Social media can create online reporting that is the equivalent of the United Way's posting of thermometers in town squares to measure giving. Only now they can be viewed by anyone and updated regularly and in an instant. America's Giving Challenge used a leader board to provide real-time information to the participants about the number of friends and funds they had raised on a particular day and overall. This added to the urgency of the contest and provided additional incentive and momentum to the participants to maintain or improve their positions.

- **Spread out the giving**. To date, donations via social networks have had low average gift amounts. This is due, in part, to the donations from younger people who have not reached their peak earning years. Gifts of $5 or $10 are quite common online. We expect that as the age of social network users increases, larger amounts will be donated online.[23]

- **Donor recognition**. Thankfulness doesn't just happen at the end of an effort. Social media, like blogs, are the perfect tools to share stories about the work people are doing on the organization's behalf in real time and create momentum for the effort. Organizations can highlight cases of individual giving that are compelling to the network. Moreover, highlighting influencers strategically spreads news about how and why people are contributing to the cause, while also encouraging those influencers' friends to do the same.

- **Storytelling lives on**. Although a particular online fundraising activity may be short-lived, the stories about the results live on, becoming part of the relationship building and credibility that organizations create with their networks over time. Take, for example, Red Nose Day 2009, a daylong fundraising event in the U.K. that raises money for people in need in the U.K. and Africa. Six months after the March 2009 event, the organization was still updating their Twitter and Facebook streams with stories about the day that will become part of the narrative of preparing for next year's day.[24]

CONCLUSION

It is important for organizations to keep reminding themselves that we are all at an early stage in learning how to turn friends into funders online. We should also take a moment to think about how to raise friends first, and focus on cultivating and nurturing those relationships in potential fertile channels such as Facebook.

Lastly, although it takes time and patience to turn friends into funders, it can be great fun as well, with organizations and free agents finding new and creative ways to energize and engage supporters for their cause. And even if the tools look different from before, the fundamentals of fundraising remain: The cause has to be compelling and urgent, and the powerful art of storytelling, now amplified with social media, has to be employed.

REFLECTION QUESTIONS

- How well do your fundraising activities on social networks connect and support your other channels?

- What are your touch points with current and potential supporters who connect with you via social networks and social media? Are you connecting with them beyond just asking for donations or asking them to vote, click, or send money? Is every contact an ask?

- Does your organization share stories about the impact of its work from a personal perspective?

- Does your organization share stories about new donors who have given to your organization through social networks? Are you identifying and cultivating donors who are influencers?

- Do your stories tug at the heartstrings or evoke an emotional reaction? Are they funny, sad, endearing, unusual?

- Do you facilitate supporters sharing their stories about your organization?

- How do you recognize, celebrate, and thank supporters for their contributions?

- Are you keeping your presence and engagement ongoing beyond the life of the campaign?

Governing Through Networks

Governance is crucial to organizational success. It is the mechanism by which outsiders can train a critical eye on operations and provide expertise, connections, and financial support. Governing boards exist primarily to safeguard organizations and develop pathways forward into an uncertain future. Unfortunately, a significant amount of data suggests that boards are not performing these functions well.

These data indicate deep dissatisfaction by nonprofit executives and board members with the effectiveness of their boards. Research also shows a growing chasm between governing boards and the organizations they serve. Yet assumptions persist about what boards should look like and how they should be structured—even as they prove ineffective at guiding organizations. This ossified vision and mutual unhappiness adds up to duty-bound performance, with too many boards simply serving as rubber stamps to staff members.

Using social media well can enable governing boards and organizations that are stuck in the past to connect to broader communities of people for input and guidance. In this chapter, we will discuss why the gap between boards and organizations makes them ineffectual, and outline ways that social media can open up governance, make it more representative of the communities the organizations serve, and better guide organizations.

We will begin by comparing the experiences of a traditional, low-functioning board with a projection of a board that works more like a social network.

TWO SCENARIOS FOR GOVERNANCE

Here is an all-too-familiar board meeting scenario:

Every morning Joe opens his desktop calendar to review his appointments and ready himself for the day ahead. Today's noon meeting gives him a familiar sinking feeling—one he has on every first Thursday of the month when it's time for Everytown's Save Our River board meeting. Joe knows from his two years on the board that today's meeting will unfold in a manner identical to the eight previous meetings.

Save Our River board meetings take place in the dark paneled conference room of August, Regal & Venerable where Henry Robbins, the board chair, is a partner. As the founding board chair, Henry is serving his fourteenth year in that position. Joe thinks of him as the organization's ruling monarch.

Every meeting is a finely orchestrated piece of Kabuki theater. Every person knows precisely what to do and when to speak and even where to sit. Generally nothing spontaneous or surprising happens. In particular, uncomfortable truths—such as the shrinking attendance at the organization's largest event, the annual cleanup day—are avoided.

Henry passes out the agenda: a welcome statement by Henry, the executive director's update, the fundraising committee's report, the treasurer's report, old business, new business, approval of minutes, and adjournment. Joe finds old business a particularly tedious twenty-minute experience. It is the catchall category for circular conversations about recruiting new board members and the regular appeal to board members who still need to give their annual contributions. Since actually naming names would be impolite and discomforting, Henry gives his practiced and polite soliloquy on the need for everyone to pitch in and support Save Our River.

Joe's main job, as with the other fourteen trustees, is to solemnly nod and agree with the big three: Henry, the treasurer Roy Fuller, and in particular, the true power source, Sandra Holloway, the founder and executive director. The unspoken rule of the board is that Sandra gets what Sandra wants, based on the reasoning that she does the actual day-to-day work.

Joe was initially very excited to join the board, and he still admires the organization. It became clear once he joined, however, that a board member's only real job is to ask their friends to write checks for the organization. In good faith, Joe initially tried to rally some friends to donate, but his heart really wasn't in it. Now he tries to contribute at board meetings and waits for his tenure to be over.

Now let's imagine how Save Our River's board could function as part of a Networked Nonprofit:

Today's Save Our River board meeting is conducted using a hybrid format that combines a face-to-face with an online meeting. The board produces the online component with a simple Web camera to broadcast the meeting. But this isn't just a one-way broadcast. People anywhere can participate in the meeting through the chat function or via an ongoing conversation about the meeting on Twitter. A tech-savvy volunteer has offered to help monitor these channels and answer any technical questions.

Joe remembers the last meeting, when there were so many messages on Twitter about the board meeting that the discussion became one of the hottest topics across the entire network. In fact, ten participants in that Twitter conversation joined the organization's young professionals group as a result.

Joe has been working with an ad hoc committee of nine people on the problem of new biofuel additives that are showing up in fresh water estuaries along the coast and running into their river. Participating in several video conferences with board members and others about this growing problem has energized Joe. As a result, Joe's committee has spent the last several months gathering data and research on the topic, using a wiki to store and share the information and develop a plan of action together.

They are also discussing ways to connect with experts on this topic, some of whom may want to participate only in the discussions and others who may want to join the board in the future. The committee members use their contacts on LinkedIn and Twitter to search for the specific skill sets they need. Joe is pleased to have recruited three world-class biofuel experts to participate in today's board meeting virtually.

A few hours before the meeting, Joe receives a message from Sally Rundgren on Twitter. She's very interested in joining today's meeting, she writes. Great, Joe thinks, Sally can lend her expertise as a leading video game designer for smart phones. The board had discussed at the last meeting the need to recruit an advisor for a new mobile engagement strategy. They want to explore developing an iPhone application for people that cleans a virtual river to earn points. It would be a terrific vehicle for teaching young people about the fragile ecological state of the river while also introducing them to Save the River.

At noon Joe enters the in-person meeting and sees that the chat discussion and Twitter messages are projected on the boardroom wall. Board chair Nancy

Bracken calls the meeting to order. Fifteen board members are present at the meeting, with many more people participating through the chat stream—about fifty attendees in total. Some attendees were recruited by board members, while others simply heard about the meeting online and decided to attend.

Nancy begins the meeting by asking the virtual participants to put their location on a Google map on the organization's Web site so that everyone can get a sense of the group's geographic diversity. This is particularly important for Save Our River since the areas in greatest need of cleanup have disproportionately affected a low-income community located next to an abandoned industrial paint factory. Joe is delighted to see three people participating from the local library in that neighborhood.

But the participants aren't just local residents. Joe notices that the person from India who contacted him on Facebook last week is also participating. He is a board member of a similar nonprofit organization in India. He wants to learn more about how Save Our River operates and how the organization has been able to work so adeptly with government agencies and corporations to clean up the river.

The agenda is posted on an area of the organization's Web site dedicated to governance, and has been widely shared and discussed prior to the meeting on several social media channels. The final agenda was shaped by the input and suggestions from the online community. The same Web site area also stores committee and financial reports, past board minutes, and links to other organizations and data for reference.

As the meeting continues, the online chat comes alive with conversation about the meeting and the agenda. In particular, the biofuel issue—the first item on the agenda—is hot. The plan is for Joe to present his committee's research and findings. His staff liaison will then present specific suggestions for how the organization can approach the issue. After that, another local environmental organization will discuss how it can better align its work with Save the River, while the representative from the governor's office will participate by Skype, a free video conference service, about the statewide policy agenda for clean rivers.

Nancy turns to Joe and says, "Okay, Joe, you're on!"

This scenario illustrates the variety of ways boards can open up their processes to allow more voices and more meaningful participation. A board working as a network receives new ideas and energy from people outside of the organization's walls. The connectedness that social networks offer has the potential to radically transform how boards guide and oversee nonprofits in the future.

Of course, not all boards are prepared to adopt this networked approach immediately, and will instead need to inch forward. We are in favor of this approach, as undoing such ingrained governance models isn't an easy task. Let's begin by examining why the existing approach isn't sustainable.

GOVERNANCE DISSONANCE

Several kinds of ineffective boards exist. One is the Rubber Stamp Board, where the board is expected to approve the plans and wishes of the staff. Muddle-Through Boards lack strong leadership at both the board and staff levels. Fiduciary Boards are almost entirely focused on financial statements and budgets.

All types share these characteristics: a lack of diversity, poor leadership, and a closed culture that doesn't allow for real discussion and outside input. Shockingly, board composition has not changed discernibly by gender, race, and profession over the past several decades. Research shows the following:

- Nonprofit governing boards are 86 percent White, 7 percent Black, 3 percent Hispanic, 2 percent Asian, and 2 percent Other.[1]

- The larger the budget of an organization, the larger the percentage of men as members.[2]

- For organizations whose constituents are more than 50 percent African American, their trustees are 18 percent African American. For organizations whose constituents are over 50 percent Hispanic or Latino, 32 percent have no Hispanics or Latinos on their board.[3]

Friends continue to recruit friends, and organizations are happy to have them. The result is that boards tend to be tight social cliques of like-minded people often from the same social backgrounds. A country club analogy is inevitable.

Stagnant board composition creates a large and growing chasm between governing boards, organizations, and the communities they serve. Judy Freiwirth, a national expert on and consultant to nonprofit boards, writes, "How can boards engage in true meaningful work, and make effective governing decisions based on a changing environment, if they are almost completely out of touch with the people they represent?"[4]

The performance of these homogeneous boards is also poor. For instance:

- Eighty percent of board members joined because the organization's mission fits their personal interests. However, only 36 percent have needed professional skills, and only 18 percent have expertise in the organization's field.

- CEOs give their boards C+ on strategic planning and monitoring organizational performance, understanding the board's roles and responsibilities, community relations, and outreach.

- The same CEOs give their boards a C on fundraising. Another study described 29 percent of boards as "very active" in fundraising, while 35 percent were ranked as "not at all active."[5]

These kinds of results led the research team of Chait, Ryan, and Taylor to ask, "Why is there so much rhetoric that touts the significance and centrality of nonprofit boards, but so much empirical and anecdotal evidence that boards of trustees are only marginally relevant or intermittently consequential?"[6]

Board members are generally polite people who want to fit in, creating cultural norms of deference to the chair that ensure that the boat never rocks.[7] As a result, too much power is concentrated in the hands of too few officers. Nothing really happens at these board meetings because nothing is supposed to happen. But something *needs* to happen because it's difficult for organizations to navigate the swirling waters of uncertainty without good governance. Someone has to decide about the future of organizations. So who is leading the way? Staff.

The rise in nonprofit organizations with professional staff has flipped the roles of board and staff. Boards have become less powerful and more technocratic as professional staffs drive strategy. Chait, Ryan, and Taylor write about this historic juncture: "The real threat to nonprofit governance may not be a board that *micromanages*, but a board that *microgoverns*, attentive to a technical, managerial version of trusteeship while blind to governance as leadership."[8]

This is not to presume or infer that staff intentions are bad. It is simply very difficult for anyone immersed in an organization to take the larger view and spot the trends and events that highlight successful paths forward. In addition, staff people are invested in maintaining their own livelihoods, making them unreliable advocates for changing organizational direction. As David Renz, a scholar of nonprofit board governance, writes, ". . . governance is a function, and a board is a structure."[9]

Often, board composition and performance is stuck because organizations presume they have little to no choice in how they are organized and operate. However, following Robert's Rules of Order is a choice, not a requirement. Organizations can also make a choice to open up their boards to a more networked approach.

GOVERNING IN NETWORKED WAYS

In *Reframing Governance*, David Renz argues that community problem solving must take place at the "meta-organizational level." Couple Renz's argument with the underwhelming performance of traditional boards, and the need for organizations to reposition their governance efforts, takes on greater urgency. And for added measure, the outward pull of social media is blurring boundaries for all parts of organizations, including boardrooms.

We recognize how unsettled nonprofit organizations can feel at this point. Using the terms *governance* and *social networks* in the same sentence can sound frightening. We have heard executive directors say that using a blog to discuss a new program or fundraising event is fine, but using Twitter to report on board meetings in real time is crazy. Looking for board members by contacting strangers on LinkedIn, or asking the crowd to elect new board members, or posting the organization's mission on Facebook and asking for input? Never! But the need to govern differently is too great for organizations to let unfounded fears paralyze them.

Organizations and their boards should engage with their ecosystems, the people who know the most about their work, to chart their course. These voices and conversations are not peripheral to governance discussions, but a fundamental part of the way organizations manage their futures. Organizations can start the conversations using whatever channels they're most comfortable with, and it will inevitably lead to more conversations and more opportunities for input.

The notion of networked governance builds on the practice of peer-to-peer governance processes that have worked well in the development of open source software projects such as Linux and Drupal. According to the P2P Foundation, the key characteristics of these governance processes include

- **Anticredentialism**, the idea that anyone can participate regardless of their title or position.
- **Collective choice systems**, meaning that the group makes key decisions democratically.

- **Communal validation**, in which the products and choices of the group are open to public scrutiny and revision.

- **Open development**, which eschews closed doors and hiding places. The entire project is developed transparently.[10]

Peer-to-peer governance principles have been applied to online communities as well as networks of organizations. They can also inform and guide the opening up of governance practices of individual nonprofit organizations.

GOVERNING AS A NETWORK: A BEGINNING

Governing boards can begin to work in networked ways without any changes to their board structure. Here are some ways in which governing boards can act more like social networks:

- **Create a private social network.** Boards should practice sharing information online and having conversations directly with one another, not just through the chair. Ning is a free online tool that creates private social networks for exactly this purpose. Online networks also enable shy board members to participate in conversations they might be uncomfortable joining in person.

- **Join a public online social network.** Love Without Boundaries, an all-volunteer organization, has a governing board of seven people. All seven of them have Facebook profiles and are members of the Love Without Boundaries Facebook page. There, board members can have more casual conversations. It also enables them to serve as ambassadors for the organization with other people on Facebook.

- **Create an open invitation to board meetings.** Announce board meetings on the organization's Web site and invite anyone to attend. These attendees don't have to be relegated to wallflower status, either; they can participate in the conversation without having a vote. Provide a conference call number to allow anyone to phone in and listen to the board meeting. Broadcast the meeting live online. Of course, boards still have the right to meet in executive sessions to discuss sensitive matters like personnel, but most conversations would be enriched with more voices.

- **Post draft agendas online.** Boards can open up their agendas to the suggestions of other people. These agendas should also have some open space, opportunities for brainstorming and creative thinking to let members wander and think together. Marching lockstep through a set agenda is part of the mentality that makes board meetings and their outcomes fait accompli in too many boardrooms.

- **Train board members in social media and network weaving.** Organizations should expect all board members to be, or be willing to become, facile with the social media toolkit so they can engage in discussions about the organization and its work online. After all, network weaving is not part of just one job description. If all board members become network weavers, they can start and facilitate conversations across multiple channels.

- **Meet somewhere new.** Board meetings don't have to happen inside boardrooms. The board could meet at the public library, school, or community center to make attending the meetings more convenient for other people.

- **Share information and data.** Organizations should create a new default setting of sharing as much information with the public as possible. The more information outsiders have, the better they can provide assistance. Withholding vital information, such as financial statements and audit reports, marginalizes the public. We have heard the concern from organizations that sharing sensitive information, such as a budget showing an organization is underperforming, will damage their fundraising. But in our experience people respond generously when organizations they care about need help. They don't respond when they feel shut out and inconsequential.

In addition to these changes in habits, organizations can consider structural changes to open themselves up to their networks. For example, in fall 2009, the American Jewish Committee chose to switch from standing committees to all ad hoc committees at both the national and local levels. This gives the Committee greater flexibility in terms of what issues the boards will focus on each year. It unlocks them from having the same conversations year after year, and allows them to create ad hoc programs that are of greater immediate interest to their network members.

Ultimately, these changes need to culminate in better and more effective governance. Chait, Ryan, and Taylor describe three modes of governance in *Governance as Leadership*: fiduciary, strategic, and generative. Effective governing boards, according to the authors, are adept at all three modes. We are familiar with fiduciary and strategic modes, but what does generative governance mean?

The generative mode is the process of looking outward and making sense of the world as it is and as it will be. It is not intended to focus on developing new services or products. Rather, it is intended to orient an organization to its ecosystem, help it to understand evolving changes and trends, and grapple with a world that is increasingly fluid and connected.

Using a networked approach to governance enables generative thinking because it allows more people to provide different perspectives about an organization's work and the state of the world around it. Let's imagine networked governance working in a generative way.

Sharon works for City Jobs in River City, an organization that trains inner city youth for technology jobs. Sharon has attended the three trainings on social media and network weaving that City Jobs offered in conjunction with their sister agency, Jobs for All, also based in River City.

As part of the last training, Sharon brainstormed with the other board members and volunteers on topics she would like to weave. She is most interested in how to keep young people in River City after high school.

The group thinks about what kinds of people need to be part of this conversation: young people, the high schools, the Chamber of Commerce, big chains like Target and Home Depot, congregations watching their membership age, and the city council seeing its tax base dwindle.

When Sharon gets home from the last training, she e-mails people she and the other training attendees know who represent these groups. She asks if they'd like to be in a conversation about how to make River City more attractive for young people, and who else should be a part of the conversation. She hears back from half of the twenty-two people that she e-mails, and in those responses learns about ten other groups and people interested in, affected by, or working on this topic.

One mentions a local blog dedicated to this topic. Another points out that the mayor's assistant on economic development has a working group on the topic, and they should connect. Sharon feeds back to the group everything she has heard, and asks if the group thinks that a blog on the topic is a good idea. Not a blog, several say, but how about a conversation on MySpace, where so many of the young people they want to reach hang out?

These conversations continue online and at board meetings. The results are greater clarity and insights. The organization can connect with more people who have a variety of experiences and ideas to share. Perhaps a specific program or activity emerges, or perhaps it doesn't. That isn't the point. The goal of these conversations is to connect Sharon and her group to the larger ecosystem in River City around this issue and to figure out the best ways—collectively—to change the polarity of young people leaving after high school.

CONCLUSION

Organizations must challenge their assumptions about their board composition, who they have invited onto their boards, and why. What's more, they need to realize they are accountable to their communities, not just acting on their behalf. Meanwhile, boards should think about their function differently, but they can only do that if they are fundamentally composed of different kinds of people. Either way, it's time to get out of the boardroom and into the community.

Governing as networks fills the chasm between boards and the communities their organizations serve by engaging people from their ecosystem who know more about the work and the community than traditional board members. It helps staff to focus their efforts on the future, not just on the pressure-packed present. Organizations can get unstuck from their governance habits—with some courage, a lot of perseverance, and the goodwill of board members and community participants willing to try to work together differently.

REFLECTION QUESTIONS

- What information about the results of your organization can you share via social media?

- What program information or fundraising strategy information can you share in the early stages to get feedback, test concepts and ideas for programs, and so on earlier in the development process?

- What changes in your bylaws do you need to make your board more accessible?

- What is the social media savvy of your board now? Who on the board can model the use of social media to govern?

- Whom else that you've encountered via social networks can you involve in your organization's governance process?

- Is your nominating committee looking for new blood through "friends" of existing board members, or on such places as LinkedIn? Is your board even on LinkedIn? Are they using it for professional networking on behalf of your organization?

CONCLUSION

We are often asked to predict the future of nonprofit organizations and social media. This is, of course, an impossible task. The future is never a linear pathway forward from where we stand right now. The future of social media is particularly inhospitable territory for prognostication because individual social media creators and users so easily shape it.

Still, we do know a few things about the future.

We know power will continue to shift away from institutions and toward individuals. Social media use will continue to spread, meaning that people's ability to connect with one another, create and share content, and organize for causes will also expand. Nonprofit organizations will use social media, make mistakes, learn from them, share their experiences, build relationships, and reinvent nonprofit organizations as they go. And we know that the passion that people have for righting wrongs and supporting people and communities will never go out of fashion.

As the American humorist James Thurber wrote, "It is better to know some of the questions than all of the answers." We are interested in continuing to try to answer these questions in the future:

Marnie Webb, the co-CEO of TechSoup Global, asked, "**What, if anything, does all of the clicking, blogging, and "friending" add up to in the end?**"[1] We know millions of people use social media to connect with one another around causes, but exactly what difference does it make? Does it help more people in need? Does it pass better laws? Does it fund more medical research? It is too soon to tell whether and how the outcomes of Networked Nonprofits differ from their predecessors, but not too soon to ask the questions and try to determine the answers.

163

Will foundations and other grantmakers invest in networks rather than organizations? Funders have primarily supported one organization at a time or a formal collaboration of several organizations—a very different model from funding a network of organizations and individuals. The David and Lucile Packard Foundation, among other foundations, has taken a deeper look at this question about how best to support networks of nonprofit organizations.[2] The Case Foundation has experimented with various creative funding strategies to leverage support to nonprofit organizations and hone their own social media skills and strategies. But these are just two examples; more foundations need to explore this territory as well.

How will Millennials behave as they take charge of organizations? Millennials such as Ben Rattray, the founder of Change.org, and Stacey Monk, the cofounder of Epic Change, are creating their own Networked Nonprofits. But how will Millennials reimagine traditional organizations as they inherit them? Will they lose their zeal for turning organizations inside out as the gravitational pull of risk-averse institutions takes them captive? Or will they flatten them and open them up to the world in ways we haven't even imagined?

In recent history, nonprofit organizations have veered toward keeping their organizations behind closed doors. Some have worked hard to keep their communities and constituents at a distance by pushing out messages and dictating strategy without listening or building relationships. These habits and missteps hurt and limit organizations and their communities. We have the opportunity now to change this trajectory.

To change course, the first and perhaps hardest step is for organizational leaders to overcome their fear of losing control. Social media flatten the world; they also make it less predictable and controllable. Nonprofit leaders can thrive in this new world by transitioning from stand-alone entities to social networks energized by abundant resources in their ecosystem.

However, even if you made it this far in this book, getting started can still feel overwhelming. We recommend these first steps for organizational leaders to get unstuck and begin their journey into a networked world:

Find a friend. As mentioned in Chapter Seven, "Making Nonprofit Organizations Simpler," it is important for people who are inching their way into social media to have a mentor who can act as their guide.

Trust your staff. One barrier to letting go for organizational leaders is learning to trust their own staff. The default setting for organizations has to shift from control and mistrust to that of trust. Having social media policies guides staff on what is expected of them and what is acceptable behavior. Hold internal discussions about the policies and expectations of staff, and clarify any misperceptions they may have. Beyond that, though, organizations need to let staff go to have conversations with people without a script. Relationships can only be built through personal connections. Staff and volunteers will make mistakes in public. They will get their facts wrong or promise something they can't deliver. Mistakes happen, but only rarely are they significant. What is fatal to organizations is cutting themselves off from their ecosystems and pretending they can solve problems alone.

Model the change. If you want to be a Networked Nonprofit, you have to behave like one. Modeling ensures that change seeps into an organization. Organizations need a few people to establish the cultural norm of transparency, building relationships, working with the crowd versus ignoring them, and above all, learning.

Try an experiment. Organizations cannot transform themselves overnight, but they can find small, safe places to experiment with working differently. Organizations can identify one fundraising event, one conversation to facilitate, or one effort that could use a crowd's help to experiment with listening, engaging with their community, and learning how to work in social ways. Try just this one thing, learn from it, and then try another.

While no timetable exists for changing an organization, it's urgent to begin. Stand-alone organizations may survive financially in the future; their relevance, however, will wane as more organizations and people recognize that working as networks is more effective.

We are as eager as our readers to know the answers to these questions. We are also excited to hear your questions. We hope the readers of this book and our blogs will join us at **www.networkednonprofit.org** to continue the conversation and share their stories and what they've learned.

As our journey continues to unfold, we will continue to watch, act, and learn with nonprofit organizations working as social networks. We will continue to chronicle their adventures, successes, and missteps as they find new, exciting, invigorating, and effective ways to build strong communities.

NOTES

CHAPTER ONE

1. Beth Kanter, "Mapping Your Online/Offline Activism: Surfrider Foundation," Beth's Blog, posted on April 6, 2009, at **http://beth.typepad.com/beths_blog/2009/04/mapping-your-onlineoffline-activism-surfrider-foundation.html** (accessed on August 2, 2009).

2. Peggy Padden, private e-mail correspondence with Allison Fine, September 18, 2009.

3. Beth Kanter and Allison Fine, "The Giving Challenge: Assessment and Reflection Report," The Case Foundation, June 22, 2009, **http://www.casefoundation.org/case-studies/giving-challenge/key-results** (accessed on September 15, 2009).

4. The Pew Internet and American Life Project (**http://www.pewinternet.org**) houses a variety of studies and research papers on the reach and use of social media in the United States.

5. Clay Shirky, *Here Comes Everybody: The Power of Organizing Without Organizations*, London: Penguin Press, 2008, page 105.

CHAPTER TWO

1. National Center for Charitable Statistics, U.S. Nonprofit Sector Overview, **http://nccs.urban.org/statistics/index.cfm** (accessed on October 2, 2009).

2. Independent Sector, "Facts and Figures about Charitable Organizations," updated October 30, 2009, **http://independentsector.org/programs/ research/research.html** (accessed on September 25, 2009).

3. Theda Skocpol, *Diminished Democracy: From Membership to Management in American Civic Life*, University of Oklahoma Press, Norman, Oklahoma, 2003, page 219.

4. David Renz, "Reframing Governance," *Nonprofit Quarterly*, Winter 2006, page 8.

5. The Bridgespan Group, "Finding Leaders for America's Nonprofits," June 30, 2009, **http://www.bridgespan.org/finding-leaders-for-americas-nonprofits .aspx** (accessed on July 13, 2009).

6. Francis Kunreuther, Helen Kim, Robby Rodriguez, *Working Across Generations: Defining the Future of Nonprofit Leadership*, Jossey-Bass/John Wiley & Sons, San Francisco, 2009, page 10.

7. The Center for Information and Research on Civic Learning and Engagement, "2006 Youth Demographics," CIRCLE Fact Sheet, **http:// www.civicyouth.org/?page_id=154**, page 8.

8. Allison Fine, "Social Citizens[BETA]," The Case Foundation, 2008. The full paper can be downloaded at **www.socialcitizens.org**.

9. Cone Research, "Civic Minded Millennials Prepared to Reward or Punish Companies Based on Commitment to Social Causes," Cone 2006 Millennial Cause Study, Cause Marketing Forum, **http://www.coneinc.com/ Pages/pr_45.html** (accessed on June 4, 2009).

10. Corporation for National Service, "Volunteer Growth in America: A Review of Trends since 1974," Learn and Serve Clearinghouse, 2006, **http:// www.servicelearning.org/library/lib_cat/index.php?library_id=7084** (accessed on June 12, 2009).

11. Amanda Lenhart, "The Democratization of Online Social Networks," Pew Internet and American Life Project, October 15, 2009, **http:// www.pewinternet.org/Presentations/2009/19-Similarities-and -Differences-in-Online-Social-Network-Use.aspx**, slide 8 (accessed on October 23, 2009).

12. Amanda Rose, personal interview with Allison Fine, June 29, 2009.

13. Further information is available at Tyson Hunger Relief, March 5, 2009, **http://hungerrelief.tyson.com/blog/2009/3/5/would_you_pledge_to _end_hunger.aspx** (accessed on September 5, 2009).

14. danah boyd, personal e-mail communication with Allison Fine, November 13, 2007.

15. Cynthia Gibson, "Citizens at the Center: A New Approach to Civic Engagement," May 31, 2006, The Case Foundation, **http://www.casefoundation.org/ spotlight/civic_engagement/summarypage** 4 (accessed on July 21, 2009).

PART ONE
CHAPTER THREE

1. Ilana Bare, "Keeping a Bag Packed at Work: Employees Today Are More Apt to Job Hop Than Ever Before," *San Francisco Chronicle*, April 30, 1999, (accessed on October 13, 2009).

2. Jane Jacobs, *The Death of American Cities*, Random House, New York, 1960, page 68.

3. Beth Kanter, "Riffing on David Armano's Listen, Learn, and Adapt: Need Your Organization's Adaption Stories!" Beth's Blog, February 5, 2009, **http://beth.typepad.com/beths_blog/2009/02/riffing-on-listen-learn -and-adapt-need-your-organizations-adaption-stories.html** (accessed on September 23, 2009).

4. Clay Shirky, *Here Comes Everybody*, 2008, Penguin Press, New York, page 125.

5. Leisa Reichelt, "Ambient Intimacy," *Disambiguity*, March 2, 2007, **http:// www.disambiguity.com/ambient-intimacy** (accessed on June 23, 2009).

6. Eva Schiffer, Net Map Toolbox Web site, **http://netmap.wordpress.com/ about/** (accessed on July 21, 2009).

7. Beth Kanter, "New Twitter Tool Mailana Helps Me to Visualize Strong Ties in My Network," Beth's Blog, March 21, 2009, **http://beth.typepad .com/beths_blog/2009/03/new-twitter-tool-mailana-helps-me-visualize -strong-ties-in-my-network.html** (accessed on October 3, 2009).

8. Valdis Krebs and June Holley, "Building Smart Communities through Network Weaving," 2002, **www.orgnet.com/BuildingNetworks.pdf** (accessed on May 1, 2009).

CHAPTER FOUR

1. Beth Kanter, "The Red Cross Created a Social Culture with Listening: Now, a Policy and Operational Handbook to Scale," Beth's Blog, July 6, 2009, **http://beth.typepad.com/beths_blog/2009/07/red-cross-social-media -strategypolicy-handbook-an-excellent-model.html** (accessed on August 2, 2009).

2. Monitor Institute, "Working Wikily: How Networks Are Changing Social Life," posted May 29, 2008, **http://workingwikily.net/?page_id=149** (accessed on May 23, 2009).

3. Geoff Livingston, "Moving From Silos to Hives, The Buzz Bin," April 6, 2009, **http://www.livingstonbuzz.com/2009/04/06/moving-from-siloes -to-hives/** (accessed on June 12, 2009).

4. Beth Kanter, "Silos Culture Inside the Walls of Nonprofits Prevents Effective Social Media Use," Beth's Blog, April 10, 2009, **http://beth.typepad .com/beths_blog/2009/04/silos-culture-inside-the-walls-of-nonprofits -prevent-effective-social-media-use.html** (accessed on May 13, 2009).

5. Allison Fine, "Web 2.0 Assessment of the Overbrook Foundation's Human Rights Grantees," The Overbrook Foundation, September 2007, **http:// www.overbrook.org/resources/resources.html** (accessed on August 2, 2009).

6. Wendy Harman, private e-mail communication with Beth Kanter, June 12, 2009.

7. Bill Traynor, "Vertigo and the Intentional Inhabitant: Leadership in a Connected World," *The Nonprofit Quarterly*, **http://www.nonprofitquarterly .org/index.php?option=com_content&view=article&id=1384: vertigo-and-the-intentional-inhabitant-leadership-in-a-connected -world&catid=156:nonprofits-and-immigration** (accessed on August 29, 2009).

8. E. Miller, interview with Allison Fine, August 23, 2009.

9. Beth Kanter, "Guest Post by Holly Hight: When Controlling the Message Stifles Community (and Staff Morale)," Beth's Blog, August 31, 2009, **http://beth.typepad.com/beths_blog/2009/08/guest-post-by-holly -hight-when-controlling-the-message-stifles-community-and-staff -morale.html** (accessed on September 8, 2009).

10. E. Miller, interview with Allison Fine, August 23, 2009.

11. Holly Ross, "Sharing Is Caring, But It's Also Hard: Why Your Audience Won't Comment on Your Blog," NTEN Blog, May 28, 2008, **http://www.nten.org/ blog/2008/05/28/sharing-is-caring-but-its-also-hard-why-your-audience -wont-comment-on-your-blog** (accessed on January 23, 2010).

12. Matt Sharpe, private communication with Beth Kanter, June 21, 2009.

13. Blog Wiki, "Blog Wiki: Bloggers Code of Conduct," **http://blogging.wikia .com/wiki/Blog_Wiki:Blogger%27s_Code_of_Conduct** (accessed on September 22, 2009).

14. Beth Kanter, "The Red Cross Created a Social Culture with Listening: Now, a Policy and Operational Handbook to Scale," Beth's Blog, July 6, 2009, **http://beth.typepad.com/beths_blog/2009/07/red-cross-social-media -strategypolicy-handbook-an-excellent-model.html** (accessed on August 2, 2009).

15. Sharlyn Lauby, "10 Must-Haves for Your Social Media Policy," Mashable: The Social Media Guide, June 2, 2009, **http://mashable.com/2009/06/02/ social-media-policy-musts/** (accessed on July 12, 2009).

16. Beth Kanter, "Social Media Guidelines: Don't Moon People with Cameras (or at Least Hide Your Face When You Do)," June 19, 2009, **http://beth .typepad.com/beths_blog/2009/06/more-on-social-media-policies-and -nonprofits-whats-your-best-advice-for-policy.html** (accessed on July 29, 2009).

CHAPTER FIVE

1. Tom Subak and Cecile Richards, interview with Allison Fine and Beth Kanter, July 30, 2009.

2. Beth Kanter, "Organizational Social Relationship Models and Strategies," Beth's Blog, June 12, 2009, **http://beth.typepad.com/beths_blog/2009/06/ listening-leads-to-engagement-relationship-models.html** (accessed on June 30, 2009).

3. Danielle Brigida, personal communication with Beth Kanter, June 5, 2009.

4. Beth Kanter, "Guest Post by Kate Bladow: My Name Is Kate and I'm a Listener," Beth's Blog, September 29, 2009, **http://beth.typepad.com/**

beths_blog/2009/09/guest-post-by-kate-bladow-my-name-is-kate
-and-im-a-listener.html (accessed on October 4, 2009).

5. Beth Kanter, "Does Social Media Help You Be Human Through Your Computer?" Beth's Blog, August 19, 2009, **http://beth.typepad.com/ beths_blog/2009/08/does-social-media-help-you-be-human-through -your-computer.html** (accessed on September 2, 2009).

6. Joe Markman, "South Shore Organizations Get $130,000 from United Way," Patriot **Ledger.com**, February 26, 2009, **http://www.patriotledger.com/ news/x7529572/South-Shore-organizations-get-130–000-from-United -Way** (accessed on June 26, 2009).

7. Beth Kanter, "Guest Post by Valeria Maltoni: Creating Movements," Beth's Blog, July 30, 2009, **http://beth.typepad.com/beths_blog/2009/07/guest -post-by-valeria-maltoni-creating-movements.html** (accessed on August 3, 2009).

8. Danielle Brigida, personal communication with Beth Kanter, June 5, 2009.

9. Tom Watson, *CauseWired: Plugging In, Getting Involved, Changing the World*, John Wiley & Sons, Hoboken, New Jersey, 2008.

10. Stephanie McAuliffe, "Network Effectiveness Tides and Tables," Starting Out, August 25, 2009, **http://stephaniemca.blogspot.com/2009/08/network -effectiveness-tides-and-tables.html** (accessed on August 30, 2009).

11. Priscilla Brice-Weller, interview with Beth Kanter, **http://qik.com/ video/81022**, May 18, 2009 (accessed on July 21, 2009).

CHAPTER SIX

1. Information about the Indianapolis Museum of Art's dashboard can be accessed at **http://dashboard.imamuseum.org**.

2. Rob Stein, e-mail communication with Beth Kanter, October 13, 2009.

3. Ibid.

4. Guidestar, "The State of Nonprofit Transparency, 2008: Voluntary Disclosure Practices," 2009, **http://publications.guidestar.org/transparency-report/** (accessed on October 23, 2009).

5. Beth Kanter, "Transparency Camp ~FT09: Blogging and Tweeting an Open Board Meeting," Beth's Blog, August 8, 2009, **http://beth.typepad.com/**

beths_blog/2009/08/transparency-camp-west-09-live-blogging-an -open-board-meeting.html (accessed on September 3, 2009).

6. John C. Havens, interview with Chris Anderson for BlogTalkRadio, February 14, 2008, **http://www.blogtalkradio.com/transparency/2008/ 02/14/Interview-with-Chris-Anderson** (accessed on July 23, 2009).

7. University of California Museum of Paleontology, "Introduction to Porifera," **http://www.ucmp.berkeley.edu/porifera/porifera.html** (accessed on May 21, 2009).

8. Beth Kanter, "Opening the Kimono," Beth's Blog, August 3, 2009, **http:// beth.typepad.com/beths_blog/2009/08/opening-the-kimino-week-on -beths-blog-a-day-in-the-life-of-nonprofit-social-media-strategists -and-tr.html** (accessed on September 30, 2009).

9. Jacqueline Trescott and James V. Grimaldi, "Ga. Tech Chief Selected as Head of Smithsonian," *The Washington Post*, March 16, 2008, **http:// www.washingtonpost.com/wp-dyn/content/article/2008/03/15/ AR2008031501150.html** (accessed on September 16, 2009).

10. SI Web and New Media Strategy, "Process-at-a-Glance," **http://smithsonian -webstrategy.wikispaces.com/Process+at-a-Glance** (accessed on October 12, 2009).

11. Beth Kanter, "Smithsonian: Crowdsourcing an Institution's Vision on YouTube," Beth's Blog, May 25, 2009, **http://beth.typepad.com/beths _blog/2009/05/smithsonian-crowdsourcing-an-institutions-vision-on -youtube.html** (accessed on August 23, 2009).

12. Jeff Jarvis, What Would Google Do? *Collins Business*, New York, 2008, page 45.

13. Lisa Belkin, "Psst! Your Salary Is Showing," Life's Work Column, *The New York Times*, August 19, 2008, **http://www.nytimes.com/2008/08/21/ fashion/21Work.html?scp=3&sq=lisabelkin,ceosalaries&st=cse** (accessed on May 21, 2009).

CHAPTER SEVEN

1. Joan Blades, interview with Allison Fine, September 22, 2009.

2. Ibid.

3. Yochai Benkler, "Complexity and Humanity," Free Souls, September 20, 2008, **http://freesouls.cc/essays/06-yochai-benkler-complexity-and-humanity .html** (accessed on September 23, 2009).

4. Margaret J. Wheatley, *Turning to One Another: Simple Conversations to Restore Hope to the Future*, Berrett-Koehler Publishers, San Francisco, California, 2002, page 20.

5. Booz Allen Hamilton, "Victims of Success: Reducing Complexity for Nonprofits," August 30, 2006, **http://www.boozallen.com/publications/ article/10980991**, **http://www.boozallen.com/media/file/Victims_of_Success .pdf** (accessed on September 23, 2009).

6. Michele Martin, "Is the Scarcity Mentality the Biggest Barrier to Social Media in Nonprofits?" The Bamboo Project, March 18, 2007, **http://michelemartin .typepad.com/thebambooprojectblog/2007/03/killing_the_mis.html** (accessed on August 2, 2009).

7. Peter Dietz, "Competition or Collaboration?" Social Edge blog, June 23, 2009, **http://www.socialedge.org/discussions/social-entrepreneurship/ collaboration-versus-competition** (accessed on September 23, 2009).

8. Steve Lohr, "Netflix Competitors Learn the Power of Teamwork," *The New York Times*, July 27, 2009, **http://www.nytimes.com/2009/07/28/ technology/internet/28netflix.html?_r=1&scp=2&sq=netflix&st=cse** (accessed on August 12, 2009).

9. Leo Babauta, *The Power of Less: The Fine Art of Limiting Yourself to the Essential . . . in Business and in Life*, Hyperion, New York, New York, 2008.

10. Beth Kanter, "Dancefloor and Balcony: What I Learned about Emergent Online Collaboration from Eugene Eric Kim," Beth's Blog, September 25, 2009, **http://beth.typepad.com/beths_blog/2009/09/dancefloor-and-balacony -what-i-learned-about-selforganizing-groups-online-from-eugene-eric -kim.html** (accessed on October 3, 2009).

11. Bill Venners, "The Simplest Thing That Could Possibly Work, A Conversation with Ward Cunningham, Part V," Artima Developer, January 19, 2004, **http:// www.artima.com/intv/simplest3.html** (accessed on September 24, 2009).

12. Chris Brogan, "Are You a Trust Agent?" Chris Brogan's blog, June 24, 2009, **http:// www.chrisbrogan.com/are-you-a-trust-agent/** (accessed on August 23, 2009).

13. Beth Kanter, "Guest Post by David Venn: Why Organizational Simplicity Is Key to Social Media Strategy Success," Beth's Blog, September 9, 2009, **http://beth.typepad.com/beths_blog/2009/09/guest-post-by-david -venn-why-organizational-simplicity-is-key-to-social-media-strategy -success.html** (accessed on September 15, 2009).

14. Paul Lamb, "Speeding Up Innovation to Slow Us Down," ComputerWorld .com, July 10, 2009, **http://www.computerworld.com/s/article/9135400/ Opinion_Speeding_up_innovation_to_slow_us_down** (accessed on September 23, 2009).

15. Howard Rheingold, "Attention Literacy," SF Gate, April 20, 2009, **http:// www.sfgate.com/cgi-bin/blogs/rheingold/detail?entry_id=38828** (accessed on May 23, 2009).

16. Beth Kanter, "Can Nonprofit Organizations Work More Like Clouds? How?" Beth's Blog, May 15, 2009, **http://beth.typepad.com/beths _blog/2009/05/does-your-nonprofit-organization-work-like-a-cloud .html** (accessed on June 12, 2009).

17. Steve Ames, interview with Allison Fine, October 15, 2009.

18. Beth Kanter, "Guest Post by David Venn: Why Organizational Simplicity Is Key to Social Media Strategy Success," Beth's Blog, September 9, 2009, **http://beth.typepad.com/beths_blog/2009/09/guest-post-by-david -venn-why-organizational-simplicity-is-key-to-social-media-strategy -success.html** (accessed on September 15, 2009).

PART TWO

1. Arianna Huffington, speaking at Craigslist Foundation Boot Camp for Nonprofits, June 20, 2009.

CHAPTER EIGHT

1. Information available at **http://www.brooklynmuseum.org/exhibitions/ click/quick_facts.php** (accessed on August 22, 2009).

2. Information available at **http://www.brooklynmuseum.org/exhibitions/ click/podcast.php** (accessed on August 22, 2009).

3. Beth Kanter, "Arts 2.0: Brooklyn Museum Click Exhibit Results: It's Not a Contest, It's a Study in the Curation of the Crowds," Beth's Blog, June 26, 2008, **http://beth.typepad.com/beths_blog/2008/06/arts-20 -brookly.html** (accessed on August 21, 2009).

4. Amanda Rose, private e-mail communication with Beth Kanter, July 21, 2009.

5. Beth Kanter, "The Magic Tweet: Crowdsourcing Opera Analysis," Beth's Blog, August 13, 2009, **http://beth.typepad.com/beths_blog/2009/08/ the-magic-tweet-crowdsourcing-an-opera-on-twitter-.html** (accessed on September 14, 2009).

6. Katya Andresen, *Robin Hood Marketing: Stealing Corporate Savvy to Sell Just Causes*, San Francisco, California, Jossey-Bass/John Wiley & Sons, 2006, page 27.

7. Carol Adelman, private e-mail communication with Beth Kanter, June 2, 2009.

8. Carrot Mob Web site, **http://carrotmob.org/about/** (accessed on October 3, 2009).

9. Wikipedia, Sturgeon's Law, **http://en.wikipedia.org/wiki/Sturgeon%27s _law** (accessed on October 23, 2009).

CHAPTER NINE

1. James O'Malley, "HSUS YouTube User-Generated Competition Grows List," Frogloop, posted March 3, 2008, **http://www.frogloop.com/care2blog/ 2008/3/3/hsus-youtube-user-generated-video-competition-grows-list .html** (accessed on September 2, 2009).

2. Carie Lewis, private e-mail conversation with Beth Kanter, August 1, 2007.

3. Alexandra Samuel, "Scoring with Social Media: 6 Tips for Using Analytics," Harvard Business Publishing, September 21, 2009, **http:// blogs.harvardbusiness.org/cs/2009/09/scoring_with_social_media_6 _ti.html** (accessed on September 30, 2009).

4. Wendy Harman, private conversations with Beth Kanter, February 2008.

CHAPTER TEN

1. charity: water, **www.charitywater.org** (accessed on September 4, 2009).

2. Tom Watson, *CauseWired: Plugging In, Getting Involved, Changing the World*, John Wiley & Sons, Hoboken, New Jersey, 2008, page 156.

3. Holly Hall, "Contributions to Big Charities Drop as Groups Struggle to Recruit Donors," *The Chronicle of Philanthropy*, April 23, 2009, **http:// philanthropy.com/premium/articles/v21/i13/13002201.htm** (accessed on August 15, 2009).

4. Pew Research Center for the People and the Press, "Haiti Dominates Public's Consciousness: Nearly Half Have Donated or Plan to Give," January 20, 2010, **http://pewresearch.org/pubs/1469/public-following -haiti-donations-texts** (accessed on January 25, 2010).

5. Beth Kanter, "Hello Washington Post: Dollars per Facebook Donor Is Not the Right Metric for Success," Beth's Blog, April 22, 2009, **http://beth .typepad.com/beths_blog/2009/04/hello-washington-post-dolllars-per -facebook-donor-is-not-the-right-metric-for-success.html** (accessed on September 22, 2009).

6. Beth Kanter, "Study Provides Baseline for Nonprofit Use of Social Networks," Beth's Blog, May 8, 2009, **http://beth.typepad.com/beths_blog/ 2009/05/port-social-networking-study.html** (accessed on September 22, 2009).

7. Allison Fine, "Washington Post Disses Facebook," A. Fine Blog, comment posted by Ivan Booth on April 22, 2009, **http://afine2.wordpress.com/2009/04/22/ wash-post-disses-causes-on-facebook/** (accessed on September 4, 2009).

8. Beth Kanter, Beth's Blog, "Four Things I Learned from NTEN Ask Expert Joe Green from Causes (and One Thing I Didn't)," **http://beth.typepad.com/ beths_blog/2009/08/four-things-i-learned-from-nten-ask-expert -with-joe-green-from-causes-and-one-thing-i-didnt.html** (accessed on September 21, 2009).

9. Rob Birgfeld, "A Facebook Success Story from the Lupus Foundation of America," Smart Blog on Social Media, July 28, 2009, **http://smartblogs.com/ socialmedia/2009/07/28/a-facebook-success-story-from-the-lupus -foundation-of-america/** (accessed on September 10, 2009).

10. Beth Kanter and Allison Fine, "The Giving Challenge: Assessment and Reflection Report," The Case Foundation, June 22, 2009, **http://www .casefoundation.org/case-studies/giving-challenge** (accessed on September 15, 2009).

11. Beth Kanter, "How Do You Measure the Success of Dog-to-Person Fundraising on Social Networks? Dollars or Doggie Treats?" Beth's Blog, February 15, 2009, **http://beth.typepad.com/beths_blog/2009/02/how -do-you-measure-the-success-of-dog-to-person-fundraising-on-social -networks-dollars-or-doggie-tre.html** (accessed on October 14, 2009).

12. Peter Dietz, "How Will Your Nonprofit Raise Money in 2012?" My Social Actions, November 20, 2008, **http://my.socialactions.com/profiles/blogs/ how-will-your-nonprofit-raise** (accessed on May 5, 2009).

13. Beth Kanter, "Pop Tech Fellows Program: Reflections," Beth's Blog, October 20, 2009, **http://beth.typepad.com/beths_blog/2009/10/poptech-fellows -program-reflections.html** (accessed on October 21, 2009).

14. C. Richards and T. Subak, interview with Allison Fine and Beth Kanter, July 30, 2009.

15. Stacey Monk, "A Conversation with Allison Fine," The Epic Change Blog, August 5, 2009, **http://epicchange.org/blog/2009/08/05/a-conversation -with-allison-fine/** (accessed on September 9, 2009).

16. Shannon Moriarity, "Choosing Streets Over Shelter," **Change.Org** Blog, End Homelessness, December 10, 2008, **http://homelessness.change.org/ blog/view/choosing_streets_over_shelter** (accessed on September 18, 2009).

17. Ben Rattray, personal e-mail to Allison Fine, September 19, 2009.

18. Valdis Krebs, "Finding the Flippers," The Network Thinker, June 14, 2009, **http://www.thenetworkthinker.com/2009/06/finding-flippers.html** (accessed on August 8, 2009).

19. Beth Kanter, "A Round Up of Food Charities and Causes to Fight Hunger," Beth's Blog, November 22, 2007, **http://beth.typepad.com/beths_blog/ 2007/11/a-round-up-of-f.html** (accessed on August 14, 2009).

20. FreeRice Web site, **http://www.freerice.com/totals.php** (accessed on September 14, 2009).

21. Help the Honey Bees, **http://www.experienceproject.com/helpthehoneybees** (accessed on September 9, 2009).

22. Beth Kanter and Allison Fine, "The Giving Challenge: Assessment and Reflection Report," The Case Foundation, June 22, 2009, **http://www .casefoundation.org/case-studies/giving-challenge/key-results** (accessed on September 15, 2009).

23. Beth Kanter, "Philanthropy 2.0 Results Published on Mashable," Beth's Blog, March 29, 2009, **http://beth.typepad.com/beths_blog/2009/03/ philanthropy-20-study-results-published-on-mashable.html** (accessed on October 12, 2009).

24. Red Nose Day Web site, **http://www.rednoseday.com/** (accessed on September 15, 2009).

CHAPTER ELEVEN

1. BoardSource, "Nonprofit Governance Index," **http://www.boardsource .org/Spotlight.asp?ID=116.369**, page 8 (accessed on May 6, 2009).

2. Francie Ostrower, "Nonprofit Performance in the United States, Findings on Performance and Accountability from the First National Representative Study," The Urban Institute, Center on Nonprofits and Philanthropy, **http:// www.urban.org/publications/411479.html** (accessed on October 12, 2009).

3. Francie Ostrower, "Nonprofit Performance in the United States, Findings on Performance and Accountability from the First National Representative Study," The Urban Institute, Center on Nonprofits and Philanthropy, **http:// www.urban.org/publications/411479.html** (accessed on October 12, 2009).

4. Judy Freiwirth, "Transforming the Work of the Board: Moving Towards Community-Driven Governance," *Nonprofit Board and Governance Review*, December 15, 2005, page 2.

5. BoardSource, "Nonprofit Governance Index," **http://www.boardsource .org/Spotlight.asp?ID=116.369**, page 6 (accessed on May 6, 2009).

6. Richard P. Chait, William P. Ryan, and Barbara E. Taylor, *Governance as Leadership: Reframing the Work of Nonprofit Boards*, BoardSource and John Wiley & Sons, Hoboken, New Jersey, 2005, page xvi.

7. Peter Dobkin Hall, "A History of Nonprofit Boards in the United States," BoardSource e-Book, 2003, page 4, **http://www.boardsource.org/ Knowledge.asp?ID=2** (accessed on May 12, 2009).

8. Chait, Ryan, and Taylor, *Governance as Leadership*, pages 4–5.

9. David O. Renz, "Reframing Governance," *Nonprofit Quarterly*, Winter 2006, page 8.

10. Peer to Peer Foundation Wiki, "Category: Governance," **http://p2pfoundation .net/Category:Governance** (accessed on May 12, 2009).

CONCLUSION

1. Allison Fine, *Social Citizens*[BETA], The Case Foundation, 2008, page 20, **http://www.socialcitizens.org/paper** (accessed on October 2, 2009).

2. Beth Kanter, "Can Networks Have Social Impact?" Beth's Blog, **http://beth .typepad.com/beths_blog/2009/10/can-networks-have-social-impact .html** (accessed on October 12, 2009).

GLOSSARY

Application: Applications are software programs that enable constructive or entertaining activities. Desktop applications can be accessed through a computer, while Web-based applications, or Web apps, are accessed through Web browsers (for example, Firefox, Internet Explorer). A popular social Web app is **Causes** (online fundraising and advocacy via Facebook).

Astroturfing: Artificial attempts at online relationship building, often done by a company or individual with an ulterior motive, such as selling products or burnishing their own reputations.

Badge: A graphic applied to a Web page. Badges are typically used as emblems promoting products, ideas, and causes and are often displayed on blogs and social network profiles. Badges with interactive features (for example, a countdown clock or an online video) are known as **widgets**. Both badges and widgets are shareable; they can be "grabbed" by other people and easily added to a new Web page through code.

Blogroll: A blogger's compilation of other blogs that are recommended sources. Blogrolls are usually listed in the sidebar of a blog.

Channels: Social media tools that are used as vehicles for conversations.

Cluster: Groups of people within a social network who are connected to one another, but who have few connections to the rest of the network.

Core: The inner group of people who do most of the work within a social network.

Crowdsourcing: Outsourcing a task to a larger group of people who each contribute to the end result. Social media tools help engage people in crowd-sourcing activities such as collecting intelligence (for example, We Are

Media), cocreation (Humane Society of the United States's PSA video contest), voting, and funding (for example, America's Giving Challenge).

Digital natives: Millennials (born between 1978 and 1993) who since birth have been exposed to the Internet and a constant stream of digital technologies.

Edge or periphery: The part of the social network that is located farthest from the core. Members of the edge are likely to be connected to other social networks.

Fortress: A type of organization that is opaque and impenetrable to outsiders.

Free agents: Individuals working outside of organizations to organize, mobilize, raise funds, and communicate with constituents for a cause. They are generally comfortable with and adept at using social media.

Hubs: Hubs are the larger nodes within networks, meaning the people or organizations that have many connections. Hubs are the influencers in the network, the people who know everyone and are known by everyone.

Influencers: People (or Web sites) who have the relative reach, influence, and social capital to mobilize others. Influence can be gauged by several metrics including the size of an influencer's network, the number of comments on his or her blog, site traffic, and so forth.

Instant messaging: Real-time text communication between one or more people via the Internet or a mobile device. While these conversations function like those in a chat room, Instant Messaging (IM) can take place in pop-up windows on a wide range of Web sites and run as independent applications (for example, Meebo).

Karma banking: Building social capital by sharing resources, time, and expertise with no expectation of an immediate return.

Ladder of engagement: A framework for deepening the relationship between an organization and its supporters. The levels of engagement are defined as follows:

- **Happy bystanders**, including blog readers, friends on Facebook, and personal acquaintances such as coworkers.
- **Spreaders**, or people who are willing to share information about a cause with other people.

- **Donors**, who contribute financially to a cause.

- **Evangelists**, who reach out to their personal social networks and ask other people to give time and money to the cause.

- **Instigators**, who create their own content, activities, and events on behalf of the cause. Instigators may even create a new cause or organization to express themselves more fully.

Leaderboard: Like their traditional counterparts, Web-based leaderboards are used to track scores, rank, or progress toward a specific goal.

Learning loops: An intentional, iterative process to monitor, understand, and improve social media efforts over time.

Listening and measurement tools: Social media tools that can help assess Web sites and online conversations. Most are available free of charge, including the following:

- **Google alerts:** Regular e-mail updates alerting when an online news article or blog post contains specified keywords (for example, the name of an organization).

- **RSS:** Real Simple Syndication (RSS) is a subscription tool used to deliver feeds (updates) from specified blogs and other Web sites. **Feedburner** is a popular tool used to track the number of subscriptions for organizational and personal blogs.

- **RSS readers:** Aggregation tools that collect feeds from all specified Web sites (e-mail is another delivery option). Popular RSS readers include **NetVibes** and **Google Reader**.

- **Search Engines:** Search engines index and rank Web sites to help Internet users find relevant content through keyword searches. Most search engines favor content that is embedded with URLs and regularly updated, tagged, and linked to from other Web sites. This content usually has greater search visibility (higher position in search results).

  - **Traditional search engines** (for example, **Google** and **Yahoo**) search all public online content (current and historical).

  - **Blog search engines** search the last six months of blogs and blog posts. **Technorati** and **Blog Pulse** are two examples of blog search engines. (**Google Blogs** will allow searches for content older than six months.)

A keyword search on Technorati yields related blogs and blog posts, and provides the blog's rank and "Authority" (the number of inbound links to that blog).

- **Message board search engines** search the last six months of discussion forums, threads, and posts. Examples include **BoardReader.com** and **Board Tracker.com**.

- **Twitter Search** allows users to search by keyword or hashtag.

- **Social bookmarking:** A way of saving and categorizing links using tags. Whereas traditional bookmarks are saved within the Web browser on a personal computer, social bookmarks are accessible from any Internet connection. Additionally, sites that help manage social bookmarks (for example, **Delicious.com** and **StumbleUpon**) allow tagged content to be searched and shared.

- **Tags:** User-generated tags allow labeling of online content with codes or keywords. Tags can be general or specific. The more often a specific tag appears (for example, WeAreMedia) the higher it will appear in search engines and social bookmarking sites. On Twitter, the tagging convention prefixes all tags with a hash mark (for example, #WeAreMedia). These **hashtags** distinguish tags from other tweeted text.

- **Tag cloud:** A weighted, visual list of tags within a specific Web site. In a tag cloud, the size of the tag is proportional to its use, with the most popular tags appearing the largest.

- **Web site analytics:** Data about a Web site's traffic, such as number of unique visitors and page views. **Google Analytics** is a robust and free analytics tool that helps analyze and optimize Web sites, including blogs. **PostRank** measures additional engagement metrics for blogs, such as comments, bookmarks, and subscriptions.

Network mapping: The process of visually drawing—or mapping—the components of a social network. (The term **social graph** was used by Facebook to describe the relationships between its members.) Strategic network mapping identifies nodes, hubs, and other connections in order to reveal opportunities to strengthen a social network.

Network weaving: Strengthening and building a social network by sharing resources, making connections, and inciting conversations.

Networked Nonprofits: Networked Nonprofits are simple and transparent organizations. They are easy for outsiders to get into and insiders to get out of. They engage people in shaping and sharing their work in order to raise awareness of social issues, organize communities to provide services, or advocate for legislation. In the long run, they help make the world a safer, fairer, healthier place to live.

Nodes: People or organizations connected in a social network.

Power law of distribution: The imbalance between the small number of people in a network who do most of the work on a project and the remaining large numbers of people who do little. It is otherwise commonly known as the 80:20 rule.

Social capital: The bundle of trust, accountability, and reciprocity that exists when relationships are meaningful and resilient.

Social change: Any effort by people and organizations to make the world a better place. It includes advocacy and direct service efforts, as well as conversations between people outside organizations about challenges that people and communities face.

Social culture: Organizational behaviors and attitudes derived from a relationship-driven focus (rather than a focus on transactions). The shift to a social culture relies on listening, participation, trust, thankfulness, and karma banking. Social media can play a significant role in enhancing a generous social culture.

Social media: The peer-to-peer communication and user-generated content made possible through the advent of participatory "Web 2.0" tools such as blogs, online social networks, multimedia sites, and text messaging. A list of different types of social media tools is included below:

- **Blogs:** Short for "Web log," a blog is a platform that allows an author (blogger) to publish content online. Blog content—whether text, photos, videos, or podcasts—is organized by categories and tags. This content is viewable on the blog in reverse chronological order in blog posts. Others can leave comments on these blog posts. Millions of blogs exist, and this sect of social media is often referred to as the "blogosphere."

- **Chat room:** A Web site that allows multiple people to communicate (chat) through real-time messages. Like listservs, most chat rooms are dedicated to specific topics.

- **Listserv:** An electronic mailing list that distributes messages to subscribers via e-mail. Listservs are usually topical and in most cases allow anyone to reply to or send a message to the group.

- **Message board:** An online community hosted in a series of topical discussion forums. Participants can post new topics via discussion threads and others can reply via comment.

- **Microblog:** According to Wikipedia, "Microblogging is a form of multimedia blogging that allows users to send brief text updates or micromedia such as photos or audio clips and publish them. . . These messages can be submitted by a variety of means, including text messaging, instant messaging, e-mail, digital audio or the web" (**en.wikipedia.org/wiki/Micro_blog**). **Twitter** is a popular microblogging platform that limits text-based tweets (posts) to 140 characters.

- **Multimedia:** Nontext-based digital content, from mp3s to videos to photos, that can be published, shared, and tagged online. Online music-sharing sites include **Napster** and **iTunes**. Online video-sharing sites include **YouTube**, **Vimeo,** and **Google Video**. Online photo-sharing sites include **Flickr**, **Picasa**, and **Piczu**.

- **Review sites:** Web sites that enable opinion sharing, ratings, and reviews, such as **Epinions** and **Yelp**.

- **Social networks:** Online communities of individuals (**nodes**) who are connected to each other via **ties** (friending, following, group membership, and so on). Social networks form through many types of social media platforms, including blog networks, listservs, and Google Groups. Larger social networks, such as **Facebook**, **MySpace,** and **LinkedIn**, serve a wide variety of interests and geographic areas. Niche social networks, such as **Change.org** and independent **Ning** networks, are typically focused on a specific topic.

- **Social news sites:** Web sites such as **Digg!** that enable people to submit and rank news stories, listing the most popular stories first.

- **Virtual World:** A computer-simulated environment—or cyber world—that enables users to interact with each other and manipulate the digital ecosytem via their personalized avatars. (**Second Life** is a well-known virtual world.)

- **Wiki:** A Web site that can be easily edited by many people simultaneously, allowing them to think together, strategize, share documents, and create plans together. Wikis help facilitate **microplanning**, the process of enabling more people to participate in the creation and implementation of an effort much less expensively over longer periods of time.

Social media policy: Organizational guidelines for participating in social media. Policies often include hard and fast rules for confidentiality, disclaimers, and disclosures in order to protect the organization, employees, and stakeholders, but should ultimately facilitate effective and authentic social media engagement. **Blogging guidelines** might include best practices. A **comment policy** might include criteria for blog comments (for example, no profanity).

Text messaging: Sending messages from one mobile phone user to another through Short Message Service (SMS), a powerful digital technology used in mobile marketing.

Ties: The connections between people and organizations, or nodes, in a social network.

Transactionals: A type of nonprofit organization that focuses primarily on selling goods and services to the public rather than relationship building. Cost is a primary selling point for these organizations.

Transparency: Honest and authentic information, communication, and actions. Transparency is a core tenet of social media engagement, requiring disclosure of affiliations and biases that—if omitted—could diminish credibility. Organizations that have transparency as a fundamental value are called **Transparents**.

URL: A Uniform Resource Locator (URL) is, quite simply, a Web address. Also referred to as links, URLs are often embedded in hyperlinked text on Web sites to direct click-throughs to other Web sites.

Viral: The organic and rapid spread of online content caused by word of mouth.

Web 1.0: The first era of the Internet, which began in the early 1990s with the advent of the World Wide Web and e-mail.

Web 2.0: The second era of the Internet, starting in the late 1990s, through which online information became inexpensively storable, shareable, and participatory through the advent of social media tools.

CHAPTER THREE

Understanding Social Networks

Easley, David, and Kleinberg, Jon. "Networks, Crowds, and Markets: Reasoning About a Highly Connected World," **http://www.cs.cornell.edu/home/kleinber/networks -book/** (accessed on January 12, 2010).

Kanter, Beth. "An Overview of Social Networking Mapping and Analysis Tools," May 29, 2009, **http://beth.typepad.com/beths_blog/2009/05/which-social-networking -analysis-term-best-describes-virgin-america.html** (accessed on January 12, 2010).

Krebs Valdis, and Holley, June. "A Brief Primer on Social Network Analysis," Orgnet.com, **http://www.orgnet.com/sna.html** (accessed on January 12, 2010).

Monitor Institute. "Working Wikily: How Networks Are Changing Social Life," posted May 29, 2008, **http://workingwikily.net/?page_id=149** (accessed on May 23, 2009).

Waddell, Steve. "Strategic Mapping and Visual Diagnostics for Scaling Change," **http:// blog.networkingaction.net/?p=271** (accessed on January 12, 2010).

A variety of free and low-cost tools can help map your friends or networks on social networking sites:

Mailiana: An application that analyzes your followers on Twitter.

Kanter, Beth. "Using Mailiana to Do a Social Network Analysis of Your Twitter Followers," March 2009, **http://beth.typepad.com/beths_blog/2009/03/new -twitter-tool-mailana-helps-me-visualize-strong-ties-in-my-network.html** (accessed on January 12, 2010).

Touch Graph: An application that maps your relationships between friends on Facebook. There is a free version with limited features: **http://www.touchgraph.com/navigator .html** (accessed on January 12, 2010).

CHAPTER FIVE

Listening, Engaging, and Building Relationships

Fleet, Dave. "The Five Levels of Social Media Responses," Social Media Today, June 8, 2009, **http://www.socialmediatoday.com/SMC/99856** (accessed on January 12, 2010).

Kanter, Beth. "Engagement Planning Worksheets," July 2007, **http://beth.typepad.com/beths_blog/2009/07/guest-post-by-alexandra-samuel-engagement-planning-work-sheets-to-engage-your-users-and-move-them-to-.html** (accessed on January 12, 2010).

Kanter, Beth. "Listening for Nonprofits in a Connected World," September 2009, **http://beth.typepad.com/beths_blog/2009/09/listening-for-nonprofits-in-a-connected-world.html** (accessed on January 12, 2010).

Kanter, Beth. "Organizational Relationship Models," June 2006, **http://beth.typepad.com/beths_blog/2009/06/listening-leads-to-engagement-relationship-models.html** (accessed on January 12, 2010).

CHAPTER SIX

Building Trust Through Transparency

Anderson, Chris. *Free: The Future of a Radical Price.* New York: Hyperion, 2008.

Bennis, Warren, Goleman, Daniel, O'Toole, James, and Biederman, Patricia Ward. *Transparency: How Leaders Create a Culture of Candor.* San Francisco: Jossey-Bass, 2008.

Fine, Allison. "Nonprofits and Transparency," November 2, 2009, A. Fine Blog, **http://afine2.wordpress.com/2009/11/02/nonprofits-and-transparency/** (accessed January 21, 2010).

Fritz, Joanne. "Best Links: Nonprofit Transparency to Reducing Donor Attrition," About.com, November 9, 2008, **http://nonprofit.about.com/b/2009/11/09/best-links-nonprofit-transparency-to-reducing-donor-attrition.htm** (accessed January 20, 2010).

CHAPTER SEVEN

Making Nonprofit Organizations Simpler

Brogan, Chris. "Ten Things You Could Do Better Today," February 26, 2009, **http://www.chrisbrogan.com/10-things-you-could-do-better-today/** (accessed on January 12, 2010).

Gotlieb, Hildy. *The Pollyanna Principles*, Renaissance Press, Tucson, Arizona, 2008.

Kanter, Beth. "Information Coping Skills," June 2009, **http://www.slideshare.net/kanter/information-coping-skills** (accessed on January 12, 2010).

Kanter, Beth. "Simplicity: The First Step," May 21, 2009, **http://beth.typepad.com/beths_blog/2009/05/the-first-step-towards-being-a-networked-nonprofit-simplicity.html** (accessed on January 12, 2010).

Kanter, Beth. "Tips For Reducing Information Overload," August 12, 2009, **http://beth.typepad.com/beths_blog/2009/08/happy-information-overload-awareness-day.html** (accessed on January 12, 2010).

Wheatley, Margaret. *Turning to One Another: Simple Conversations to Restore Hope to the Future.* San Francisco: Berrett-Koehler, 2002.

CHAPTER EIGHT
Working with Crowds

Brabham, Daren C. "Get Ready for Crowdsourcing," August 2009, **http://henryjenkins .org/2009/08/get_ready_to_participate_crowd.html** (accessed on January 12, 2009).

Brabham, Daren C. Research on crowdsourcing, **http://darenbrabham.com/** (accessed on January 12, 2010).

Howe, Jeff. *Crowdsourcing: Why the Power of the Crowds Is Driving the Future of Business.* New York: Three Rivers Press, 2008.

Howe, Jeff. "Crowdsourcing: Why the Power of the Crowd Is Driving the Future of Business" (blog), **http://crowdsourcing.typepad.com/cs/** (accessed on January 12, 2010).

Kanter, Beth. "Can Crowds Be Trained Like Seals?" August 2009, **http://beth.typepad .com/beths_blog/2009/08/can-crowds-be-trained-like-seals.html** (accessed on January 12, 2010).

Kanter, Beth. "Crowdsourcing Resources for Nonprofits (Part One)," August 2009, **http:// beth.typepad.com/beths_blog/2009/08/how-does-your-nonprofit-work-with-crowds-crowdsourcing-week-on-beths-blog.html** (accessed on January 12, 2010).

Shirky, Clay. *Here Comes Everybody: The Power of Organizing Without Organizations.* London: Penguin Press, 2008.

Surowieki, James. *Wisdom of the Crowds.* New York: First Anchor Books, 2005.

CHAPTER NINE
Learning Loops

Kanter, Beth. "Listen, Learn, and Adapt," February 2009, **http://beth.typepad.com/ beths_blog/2009/02/riffing-on-listen-learn-and-adapt-need-your-organizations -adaption-stories.html** (accessed on January 12, 2010).

Kanter, Beth. "A Methodology for Learning from Social Media Projects from June Holley," September 2009, **http://beth.typepad.com/beths_blog/2009/09/a-methodology -for-learning-from-social-media-pilots-reflection.html** (accessed on January 12, 2010).

Kanter, Beth. "Real Time Analysis of Social Media Fundraising Campaign," August 2008, **http://beth.typepad.com/beths_blog/2008/08/tracking-the-fl.html** (accessed on January 12, 2010).

Kanter, Beth. "Social Media ROI Poetry Slam," March 2009, **http://beth.typepad.com/ beths_blog/2009/03/sxsw-social-media-nonprofit-roi-poetry-slam-slides-links -and-poems-long.html** (accessed on January 12, 2010).

Li, Charlene. "ROI of Blogging," November 2006, **http://blogs.forrester.com/ground -swell/2006/10/calculating_the.html** (accessed on January 12, 2010).

Social Media Metrics Wiki. **http://socialmediametrics.wikispaces.com/** (accessed on January 12, 2010).

CHAPTER TEN
From Friending to Funding

Andresen, Katya, and Strathmann, Bill. "People to People Fundraising: Crafting the Marketing Strategy to Make It Happen." In Ted Hart, James Greenfield, and Sheeraz Haji (eds.), *People to People Fundraising: Social Networking and Web 2.0 for Charities.* Hoboken, NJ: John Wiley & Sons, 2007.

Kanter, Beth. "Fundraising 2.0 Blog Posts," **http://beth.typepad.com/beths_blog/ fundraising20/** (accessed on January 12, 2010).

Kanter, Beth. "Giving Good Poke: Personal, Socially Networked Fundraising," **http:// gsp4good.wikispaces.com/** (accessed on January 12, 2010).

Kanter, Beth. "The Secrets of Social Fundraising," **http://socialfundraising.wikispaces .com/** (accessed on January 12, 2010).

Kanter, Beth, and Fine, Allison H. "The Giving Challenge Assessment and Reflection Report," The Case Foundation, June 22, 2009, **http://www.slideshare.net/kanter/ information-coping-skills** (accessed on November 12, 2009).

Schultz, Dan. "A DigiActive Introduction to Facebook Activism," DigiActive, 2008, **http:// www.digiactive.org/category/guides-resources/** (accessed on Novemer 21, 2009).

Watson, Tom. *CauseWired.* Hoboken, NJ: John Wiley & Sons, 2009.

CHAPTER ELEVEN
Governing Through Networks

BoardSource. www.boardsource.org (accessed on January 12, 2010).

Chait, Richard P., Ryan, William P., and Taylor, Barbara E. *Governance as Leadership: Reframing the Work of Nonprofit Boards.* Hoboken, NJ: BoardSource and John Wiley & Sons, 2005.

onPhilanthropy, "onLine," **http://flip.onphilanthropy.com/online/2009/11/ social-media-for-accountability-part-1-board-governance.html?utm _source=feedburner&utm_medium=feed&utm_campaign=Feed%3A+onphilan thropy%2FlYsI+%28onLine%29** (accessed on January 12, 2010).

Ostrower, Francie. "Nonprofit Performance in the United States, Findings on Performance and Accountability from the First National Representative Study," The Urban Institute, Center on Nonprofits and Philanthropy, 2007, **http://www.urban .org/publications/411479.html** (accessed on January 12, 2010).

Renz, David. "Reframing Governance." *Nonprofit Quarterly*, Winter 2006, *13*(4), 6–13.

INDEX

Made in United States
North Haven, CT
01 April 2023

34829846R00124